"For years, the treatment of dually diagnosed clients has posed a conundrum fᵒ psychiatric and substance treatment clinicians frequently advocate for treating ᵖ use disorders either separately or sequentially. Having worked in both psychiatric and substance treatment settings, I've seen the unfortunate outcomes of holding this belief. Clients feel invalidated by the people who want to help them, spend years in treatment and are often unable to build a life worth living.

In *DBT Skills Training for Integrated Dual Disorder Treatment Settings*, Lane Pederson, PsyD, LP, DBTC provides a practical model for simultaneous treatment of psychiatric and substance use disorders. Clinicians working with dually diagnosed clients will appreciate the thoughtful integration of the most effective contemporary treatment models used in both psychiatric and substance treatment; clients will appreciate the integration of these approaches in the development of easy-to-follow worksheets that reinforce key concepts of recovery."

Bari Platter, MS, RN, CNF, author of *Integrating Dialectical Behavior Therapy with the Twelve Steps*

"I want to commend Lane Pederson for the fresh and unique methodology and skills training approach described in his latest manual, "DBT Skills Training for Integrated Dual Disorder Treatment Settings". He has taken what has been used in previous models for DBT and expanded it in such an insightful way that I found myself identifying with his methods in the way I approch many of my own recovery challenges. I have been in continuous 12-Step recovery since October 1971 and have worked with dual diagnosed members using the 12-Steps to maintain abstinence with substance abuse. This manual is so resourceful that I would recommend each therapist apply these principles within their own lives in order to enhance their own ability to touch the suffering of their clients with a compassionate awareness. This manual is a unique contribution to the treatment of the dual diagnosis population, and will pave the way for a great leap forward in successful treatment modalities."

Tom Catton, author of *The Mindful Addict: A Memoir of the Awakening of a Spirit*

"As a clinician practicing Dialectical Behavior Therapy for over a decade I felt that DBT was a perfect modality for treating patients with co-occurring disorders. Reading Dr. Pederson's Skills Training Manual for Dual Disorders not only confirmed my beliefs, but the Manual provided the structure I needed to put this theory into practice. Dr. Pederson's Manual blends DBT with traditional chemical dependency treatment in a respectful and cogent manner and does so in a way that makes it easy to apply this treatment in real world settings. It truly is a resource that practitioners will use daily in their treatment of patients with co-occurring mental illness and substance use disorders."

Wade Kuehl, MSW, LISW, Clinical Director, Siouxland Mental Health Center

"Many of the clients that present for mental health or substance use problems often have the other problem as well. Clinicians are often asking how to treat both mental health and substance use problems together. This book is the answer. It provides well proven strategies to deal with substance use problems head on by utilizing one of the best evidence based strategies for this -- DBT. As a clinician, supervisor and clinical director serving clients with co-occurring disorders, I would highly recommend this book. It has improved my clinical skills, fostered the development of clinicians and most importantly lead to improved client outcomes and satisfaction."

Cathy Moonshine, PhD, MSCP, MAC, CADC III, author of *Acquiring Competency and Achieving Proficiency with Dialectical Behavior Therapy (Volumes I & II)*

"The manual provides patient handouts that target mental health and substance use symptoms simultaneously, as well as well-defined interventions based on clients' stage of change, personal values, and relapse triggers. These are excellent tools for clients whose struggles with living "in the moment" and tolerating painful emotions endanger their holistic recovery."

Annie Peters, PhD, LP, Hazelden Graduate School of Addiction Studies

Copyright © 2013 by Lane Pederson
PESI Publishing and Media
PESI, Inc.
3839 White Ave
Eau Claire, WI 54703

Printed in the United States of America

Cover and Layout Design: Matt Pabich
Edited by: Marietta Whittlesey & Kayla Omtvedt

ISBN: 978-1-93612-832-7

Library of Congress Cataloging-in-Publication Data

Pederson, Lane.
  DBT skills training for integrated dual disorder treatment settings / by Lane D. Pederson, PsyD, LP, DBTC.
    pages cm
  Includes bibliographical references.
  ISBN-13: 978-1-936128-32-7 (pbk.)
  ISBN-10: 1-936128-32-2 (pbk.)
  1. Dialectical behavior therapy. 2. Dual diagnosis--Treatment. I. Title. II. Title: Dialectical behavior therapy skills training for integrated dual disorder treatment settings.
  RC489.B4.P42 2013
  616.89'142--dc23
            2013004162

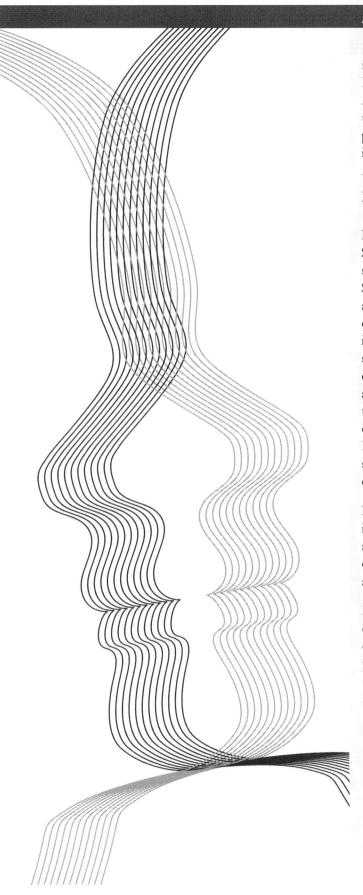

ABOUT THE AUTHOR

Lane Pederson, PsyD, LP, DBTC,
is the founder and CEO of Dialectical
Behavior Therapy National Certification and
Accreditation Association (DBTNCAA),
the first active organization to certify DBT
providers and accredit DBT programs. He
is also the author of *The Expanded Dialectical
Behavior Therapy Skills Training Manual: Practical
DBT for Self-Help and Individual & Group
Treatment Settings.*

Dr. Pederson co-owns Mental Health
Systems, PC (MHS), one of the largest DBT-
specialized practices in the Midwest United
States with multiple locations. MHS is also
an APPIC accredited training center for
clinical psychology students and interns, and
it provides training for clinical social work
students as well. At MHS, Dr. Pederson has
developed DBT programs for adolescents
and adults, has served as a clinical and
training director, and has overseen the care
of thousands of clients with co-morbid Axis
I and II disorders in intensive outpatient
settings. In addition, he has coordinated and
directed clinical outcome studies.

Dr. Pederson is a highly-rated and in-demand
international speaker and educator in DBT
and personality disorders, teaching thousands
of professionals in public and private events
across the United States and Australia.

Known as an advocate of practice-based
evidence, Dr. Pederson emphasizes
customizing treatments to diverse client
populations and using outcome data to
demonstrate clinical effectiveness and to
improve the quality of services.

DBT SKILLS TRAINING FOR INTEGRATED DUAL DISORDER TREATMENT SETTINGS

By Lane D. Pederson, PsyD, LP, DBTC ————————————

PESI
Publishing
& Media

www.PESI.com

Contents

♦ – Denotes Worksheets and Forms

◆ – Denotes Worksheets and Forms

♦ – Denotes Worksheets and Forms

Preface

Treatments for people with dual disorders[1] have long been fractured by a lack of understanding and coordination between the mental health and chemical dependency fields. Often clients with co-occurring disorders have received treatment serially and sequentially rather than in an integrated fashion, resulting in less than effective outcomes, added costs to care systems, and lost opportunities for more satisfying lives.

After specializing in DBT for well over a decade, my colleagues and I decided to embark on designing an integrated program for people requiring the skills and specialties of both the mental health and chemical dependency fields. After a prolonged period of planning and development, we launched our Integrated Dual Disorder Treatment (IDDT) program called Fusion. This program, grounded in DBT and DBT-S[2] philosophy and interventions, also sought to follow well-established guidelines on integrated treatment set forth by definitive manuals (Muesler et al., 2003) and the Substance Abuse and Mental Health Services Administration (SAMHSA).

We discovered that DBT-S, with some practical modifications and a particular emphasis on skills training and behavioral activation, was an effective fit for working with the diversity that a dual disorder population presents within clinical practice. This manual extends our practice-based work to other providers seeking a cogent, coherent, and actionable approach to helping people who struggle with co-occurring disorders develop the skills necessary to creating more satisfying lives.

The first half of this manual provides basic background on DBT-S and IDDT, starting with philosophy and contextualism and ending with practical ways of implementing a program and addressing clients' needs. The second half of the manual consists of skills training, skills plans, and worksheets to be used in treatment with clients. The over-arching goal of this manual is to make a complex treatment accessible to practitioners on the frontlines, with an emphasis on applicability over theory. My hope is that this manual exceeds that goal, and I wish you the best as you help your clients to create more satisfying lives.

Lane Pederson

---

[1] The term dual disorders is used to represent people with both mental illness and substance use disorders. The terms dual diagnosis and co-occurring disorders are used interchangeably with dual disorders in this manual. Specific disorders, except in reference to research that specifies specific disorders, are not usually named in this manual as a skills-based approach is applicable to a wide range of disorders when embedded in common therapeutic factors. This issue is discussed in more detail in the chapter that discusses contextualism and therapy.

[2] DBT-S denotes the treatment model developed by Marsha Linehan and Linda Dimeff for treating people with co-morbid borderline personality disorder and substance use disorders. DBT-S has been shown to be efficacious and the approach continues to develop. In this manual, the term DBT-S is used to describe the philosophies and interventions that constitute the treatment approach and not necessarily adherence to Linehan's service delivery framework. The terms DBT and DBT-S are also sometimes used interchangeably when referring to general dialectical behavior therapy philosophies, theories, and techniques.

Acknowledgments ——————————————

I gratefully acknowledge those at CMI Education Institute and Premier Publishing & Media for their hard work and contributions that made this manual a reality. I specifically would like to thank Linda Jackson, Kayla Omtvedt, Mike Olson, Claire Zelasko, Matt Pabich, Darren Kirby, and Mike Conner.

Additionally, I want to thank Mark Carlson, Shelley Furer, and Steve Girardeau for the encouragement to write this book, and I especially want to acknowledge Kathleen Hinton for her contributions that greatly improved the final manuscript.

Last, but most importantly, I give special thanks and appreciation to Cortney, Sophie, and Sawyer for their support during the preoccupations that came with creating this work. The love of my family eclipses all else.

Part One
EXPLANATION OF DBT-S

Introduction to DBT and DBT-S

Dialectical behavior therapy (DBT) is an empirically supported treatment for borderline personality disorder. Originally developed by Marsha M. Linehan for highly suicidal and self-injurious people in her research setting, it is safe to say that this approach has been widely disseminated into community settings, both in her original treatment model (i.e., standard DBT) and in many effective adaptations. With well over two decades of research and clinical practice in the rear-view mirror, DBT has been applied extensively to a broad spectrum of mental illnesses and has also been adapted by providers for use with substance use disorders[3] (SUD) in chemical dependency settings. In a research setting, Linehan, Dimeff, and others have studied the application of DBT with certain additions to women with borderline personality disorder and SUD (Linehan et al., 2002; Linehan et al., 1999). They have called this adaptation DBT-S.

The popularity of DBT may come from its explicit focus on acceptance and non-judgment so valued by clients and therapists along with its emphasis on behavioral activation and change so embraced by an accountability-based culture in health care. DBT combines some of the best elements of humanistic, behavioral, and cognitive approaches (Marra, 2005) along with philosophies that guide treatment and inform clients and therapists regarding what to do, when, and how (Linehan, 1993a). Additionally, the total integration of skills training in DBT provides a method for clients who want to build more satisfying lives (Linehan, 1993b).

Specific to treating substance abuse and dependence, DBT-S has expanded traditional DBT with particular philosophies and interventions to address those issues alongside mental illness (Dimeff & Linehan, 2012; McMann et al., 2007). With a solid and growing empirical basis, DBT-S promises to be a treatment of choice for co-occurring disorders.

In this manual, the reader will learn the nuts and bolts of a cogent and effective approach to clients with dual disorders. This manual is meant to supplement and not supplant Linehan's (1993a) book *Cognitive-Behavioral Treatment of Borderline Personality Disorder*. Although that book is not about the treatment of dual diagnosis per se, it is an essential source for complete explanations of DBT philosophies and interventions. Providers are strongly encouraged to study that book and the other source materials referenced in this manual.

Careful readers will find occasional differences between Linehan's and the author's viewpoints on certain subjects. While Linehan developed DBT and DBT-S in her university setting, the author has extensive experience applying these approaches in real-world community settings with diverse populations. *Readers will need to look to all the information, especially what is needed with their clients in their settings, to figure out the best dialectical synthesis.* Additionally, in the spirit of evidence-based practice, this manual will explain how other popular empirically-supported approaches relate to and can be integrated into DBT-S treatment.

In combination with Linehan's book, other readily available DBT and non-DBT resources (found in the bibliography of the book), and the empirical literature, this manual will provide therapists with the structure, framework, and skills teachings needed to conduct an effective integrated dual disorder treatment program.

---

[3] This manual uses the terms substance use and substance use disorder(s) (SUD) to refer generally to all types of substance use, abuse, and dependency problems. Occasionally, the terms chemical use, abuse, and dependency; and alcohol and drug use, abuse, and dependency are also used. The authors' intention is to be inclusive rather than exclusive with language. **Clients without particular diagnoses and issues referred to in the manual can simply be instructed to disregard those labels and descriptions in order to think about how the information and skills relate specifically to them.**

Introduction to Integrated Dual Disorder Treatment (IDDT)

IDDT refers to the thoughtful integration of mental health and substance use treatments to more effectively meet the needs of people with dual disorders.

IDDT was developed to address the shortcomings that result from the serial treatment of mental health and substance use disorders. When treated serially, people assessed with co-occurring disorders get referred to one treatment versus the other based on which condition has been determined to be "primary." Singular treatment by specialists in mental health or specialists in chemical dependency leaves the symptoms of the "secondary" disorder(s) untreated, and this often results in diminished treatment outcomes and outright treatment failures.

When the desired outcomes do not materialize, it is common for people to be referred to the other discipline based on the assumption that the untreated disorder(s) have undermined treatment success. Over time, people with dual disorders bounce back and forth between treatments. When this fractured treatment falls short there are significant and unnecessary costs to those who pay for treatment, overshadowed only by the human costs suffered by clients, their families, and the community.

To address the shortcomings of serial treatment, IDDT combines treatments so that all relevant problems can be addressed by the same provider and/or team of providers. This combined treatment approach demonstrates an understanding and appreciation for the relationship(s) between two or more co-existing disorders.

Integrated Treatment for Dual Disorders, A Guide to Effective Practice (Mueser et al., 2003) comprehensively explains the principles of IDDT. IDDT principles are also outlined by the U.S Department of Health and Human Services Substance Abuse and Mental Health Services Administration (SAMHSA). The basic principles of IDDT and how DBT-S speaks to them include:

- **Integrated Services:** Treatment of mental health and substance use disorders are combined to meet needs in a holistic manner. DBT-S is a skills-based psychosocial treatment that has wide applicability and has been researched for co-morbid conditions (e.g., Borderline Personality Disorder and SUD). Beyond traditional DBT-S, this manual encourages further integration of chemical dependency interventions and skills that are compatible with the approach.[4]

- **Cross-trained Providers:** Practitioners need to be well-trained in both chemical dependency and mental health treatments to truly integrate services. Although traditional DBT-S does not explicitly address cross-training with substance abuse treatment providers, this manual recognizes that it needs to happen for effective clinical practice. Providers from both disciplines need to be open to learning and implementing assessment and intervention techniques from the other, and even when the IDDT approach is "centered" in a particular orientation like DBT-S, there is room for adaptations that flow coherently from theory to practice (see the section on contextualism and DBT-S).

- **Stage-oriented Treatment:** Practitioners tailor treatment to clients' stage of recovery. DBT has a stage-oriented approach described later in this manual, with an emphasis in DBT-S on the pre-treatment engagement of clients. Further, a study examining the application of the transtheoretical model (TTM) of stages of change (Prochaska & DiClemente, 1983; Prochaska, DiClemente, & Norcross, 1992) to standard DBT found "that conceptualizing motivation or patient readiness-to-change in terms of the TTM stages-of-change can enrich and further our understanding of the process of change in people with BPD treated with DBT" (Soler

---

[4] The skills presented in this manual reference their application to symptoms of mental illness and substance use. Using a reference to one set of problems versus the other is not intended to emphasize or imply the primacy of one over the other.

et al., 2008, p. 424). Based on the idea that stages of treatment and stages of change can be applied to virtually any treatment model, both are explained and their use is encouraged in this manual.

- **Motivational Interventions:** Techniques used to enable clients to articulate and enact their recovery goals. Increasing the motivation of clients is a primary function of DBT. As explained later, motivational interviewing techniques can be conceptualized as dialectical in nature, and they are compatible with a DBT-S approach.

- **Cognitive-behavioral Interventions:** CBT is endorsed as the primary therapy orientation used to create change in clients' thoughts, feelings, and behaviors. DBT is an adaptation and expansion of CBT, especially in regard to expanded and systematic skills training.

- **Multiple Formats:** Services are to be provided in individual, group, family, and self-help modes. DBT-S is a multi-modal therapy by design. Standard DBT-S has five primary modes: individual, group, consultation, phone coaching, and case management. As explained later, DBT-S can be applied in other treatment formats and frameworks, although DBT-S in IDDT settings should ensure that as many of these formats as possible are available based on level-of-care determinations.

- **Integrated Medication Services:** Clients who require medications need collaborative and connected psychiatric services. DBT-S philosophy supports the integration of psychiatric services.

Readers can find more detailed definitions and descriptions of these IDDT guidelines and associated resources at www.samhsa.gov.

Getting Started: DBT-S Philosophy

Core Dialectics and Assumptions

Dialectics originated with ancient philosophers who argued that there is no such thing as an absolute position. In other words, each position on a continuum has its own truth and its own wisdom, and what seem like opposites or contradictions are related to one another. In dialectics, the search for relative truth is what leads to synthesis and balance. This synthesis and balance is particularly important when people get caught in extremes of emotions, thoughts, and behaviors. Through noting, accepting, and validating the "valid" in a particular position, the therapist and client can then fluidly move to change strategies. The movement between acceptance and change is determined by what will be effective in the context of the moment, in relation to future moments, knowing that context continuously evolves.

The most fundamental dialectic in DBT is acceptance versus change (Linehan, 1993a). It was Carl Rogers who once said, "the paradox is that when I accept myself as I am, then I can change." In DBT, we recognize that acceptance of the person, in the moment, is what opens the door to change. This tension between acceptance and change highlights the dialectical philosophy of holding two opposites at the same time. As Dimeff and Linehan (2012) have noted, the simultaneous holding of acceptance and change is synonymous with the Twelve Step philosophy captured in the Serenity Prayer: "God, grant me the serenity to accept the things I cannot change, the courage to change the things I can, and the wisdom to know the difference."

Dialectics also respect that any view of a particular situation is partial in nature, so it is important to always search for what is missing in pursuit of the most complete synthesis possible. The mutual search for synthesis shared by therapist and client keeps the treatment responsive to what works in each moment as time moves forward and the treatment evolves. There are times to accept and times to push toward change; times to stay still and times to move. The search, the validation of respective positions, and the interrelatedness and movement between the acceptance and change dialectic is a hallmark of DBT.

Another important dialectic in DBT is the belief that clients are doing the best they can, but that they also need to do better (Linehan, 1993a). This dialectic also holds true for therapists. The belief that we are doing the best we can helps us step out of our judgments and to find our compassion for others and ourselves. It is fundamentally true that we all are trying to get our wants and needs met in the best way possible. It is also true that we need to find more effective ways of reaching these goals at times. Again, by holding in mind the concepts inherent in this assumption we are able to pursue both acceptance and change.

In the effort to do better and be more effective, clients need to learn new skills and behaviors. To simply push toward change is ineffective without replacement behaviors. Therefore, it is the goal of DBT-S to continually build up clients' capabilities through skills training. Change only occurs through the acquisition and practice of skills in an accepting and validating treatment environment. In other words, the way in which the skills are taught are as important as the skills themselves.

Dialectics and Abstinence

DBT-S is an abstinence-based treatment. Similar to the goal of having clients give up suicidal behaviors, self-injurious behaviors, or other self sabotaging behaviors, DBT-S pushes for full cessation of the alcohol and drug use that is destroying clients' lives. However, complete abstinence is not a pre-requisite to entering a DBT-S program, knowing that many clients do not begin treatment with the skills needed to accomplish this goal. This treatment approach appreciates that many clients struggle with abstinence for a variety of reasons, so clients are asked to commit to sobriety knowing that it may be more of a behavioral process than a single decision. Similar to a Twelve Step philosophy, clients are asked to commit immediately to abstinence for a realistic timeframe, and then asked to recommit once they have accomplished that goal. Depending on the client, the timeframe could be one week, one day, one hour, or one minute. Many people in recovery have wisely noted, "I don't know how to stay sober for a lifetime, but I know how to stay sober for a day." DBT-S embraces this moment-to-moment approach.

Along with the assertive request that clients immediately quit alcohol and drug use, therapists also take a nonjudgmental approach to shortcomings in relapses. When clients struggle to use new skills and fall into old behaviors, therapists focus on acceptance and increasing motivation by treating a lapse as a learning opportunity. Oftentimes this is accomplished through behavioral change analysis, explained later in this manual.

Koerner (2012) has noted that this concept of dialectical abstinence, simultaneously requesting complete cessation while simultaneously learning from mistakes helps to minimize what Marlatt has called the "abstinence violation effect." That abstinence violation effect refers to the phenomenon that many people will take a relapse to an extreme. For example, someone who uses drugs who has relapsed into smoking marijuana may then decide to also do methamphetamine, or someone who has taken a drink may decide to go on a binge. Instead of falling into that trap, clients are encouraged to quickly reorient and keep moving forward with recovery. Metaphorically speaking, if you are taking a journey by horseback and fall off the horse, you would simply dust yourself off, get back on and start riding to your destination again, avoiding the same mistake that led you to fall off your horse in the first place. What you would not do, is compound your mistake by walking, running or sprinting back to your original starting point. Practically speaking, this is done by helping the client to tolerate the negative affect that frequently comes with a slip and to immediately build skills into the client's written plan to stay sober and healthy. The client may also have work to do to repair any negative consequences associated with the relapse.

In DBT-S, complete abstinence is not required as a prerequisite to treatment. Pursuant to the assumption that clients are doing the best that they can, therapists both push for abstinence and recognize that this is a goal that requires new skills and capabilities for many clients. Asking clients to perform behaviors that are not within their skill sets is fundamentally invalidating.

Dimeff and Linehan (2008) emphasize that therapists must determine the degree of abstinence that fits for each client based on the following guidelines (p. 42):

1. As determined by relevant assessment, the substance causing the most problems would be the highest target.

2. Substances that precipitate use of the most problematic substance would be the secondary target.

3. Treatment goals must be within the client's capability.

Dimeff and Linehan emphasize that clients with high co-morbidity can only change so much, so fast. Therefore, choosing to focus on only the highest- order problems, such as suicidality, or the most problematic substance may be necessary. This is similar to the DBT philosophy that one needs to radically accept having many problems in order to work on one problem. As treatment continues, lower priority problems will ultimately be addressed on the road to mental health and abstinence. The practical application of using a treatment hierarchy to determine treatment targets is discussed later.

How DBT-S is Similar To and Different From Other Approaches

This section is intended to give a brief overview of DBT in relation to other common and traditional approaches to treating SUD to highlight basic similarities and differences; it is not intended to give comprehensive descriptions of other approaches. Interested practitioners are encouraged to seek source materials for more extensive information on other treatment approaches. Additionally, practitioners should strive to integrate elements of these other approaches into the DBT approach as directed by IDDT guidelines and, most importantly, as guided by particular client needs.

Motivational Interviewing (MI) and DBT-S

Motivational interviewing (Miller & Rollnick, 2002) is a well-established approach for facilitating change, and it has been shown to be both efficacious in research and effective in practice for substance use disorders. Although motivational interviewing (MI) techniques are frequently used in individual therapy interactions, Mueser et al. (2003) have described how they can be applied in group and family settings too.

Similar to DBT-S, MI places a high value on the non-judgmental understanding of the client, although the approaches use slightly different terms and processes to reach the same goal. In DBT-S, the techniques of validation are used whereas MI emphasizes expressing empathy through active and reflective listening. In practice, the differences are mostly academic and semantic.

DBT-S and MI recognize that clients struggle with the motivation to change behaviors, and both seek to increase motivation as ultimately expressed by what a client does or will do, not by some internal construct of motivation. That said, DBT-S is explicit in defining the existence of motivation as choices made in the context of relevant behavioral techniques such as prompting, shaping, and reinforcing behaviors and through the use of behavioral contingencies. Motivating change is the essence of MI, and increasing the motivation of the client (and the therapist) has been described as an essential function of comprehensive DBT and DBT-S (Dimeff & Linehan, 2008).

In developing movement toward change, both treatments emphasize goals as important. MI aims to gather knowledge about the client, past, present, and future to elicit goals, and DBT seeks to establish goals (and methods to accomplish goals) as a part of the pre-treatment stage. An important difference is that in MI clients provide more of the direction as to what the goals are and when they are accomplished whereas DBT-S can be more directive and will explicitly guide what to address in what order as guided by the treatment hierarchy.

To accomplish goals, DBT and MI share similar strategies to highlight discrepancies between clients' stated goals and behaviors. MI seeks to have the client discover how substance use short-circuits goals in order to create a state of dissonance that will spur change. This strategy, called developing discrepancy, is like the dialectical strategy of "entering the paradox," in which the therapist highlights apparent contradictions without stepping in to solve the problem (Linehan, 1993a).

When resistance occurs (which is not uncommon with any type of client), MI and DBT use overlapping strategies. MI seeks to "roll with resistance" by not pathologizing it and instead exploring it to understand and problem-solve real barriers as well as expressing the reasons to not change in order to have the client own the arguments for change. In DBT, clients are understood using validation counter-balanced with techniques such as extending (joining with and going in the direction of the client) and playing devil's advocate (e.g., challenging the client's reasons for stopping alcohol or drug use).

Lastly, both approaches emphasize developing self-efficacy. MI adopts a strong attitude of belief and expectancy in change while also reframing difficult times and failures as demonstrations of resilience, coping, and overcoming. DBT also adopts strong belief and expectancy in clients, but an important difference is that DBT provides extensive behavioral skills training to help clients develop new capabilities along with behavioral interventions and contingencies to guide and direct them toward self-efficacy.

Readers may recognize that MI is dialectical in many of its strategies and much of it can be used compatibly with DBT-S. In fact, guidelines on IDDT set forth by SAMHSA define integrated treatment as containing both motivational interventions and cognitive-behavioral approaches. Consistent with evidence-based practice and contextualism, DBT-S therapists would be wise to integrate MI into the approach as indicated by their expertise and their clients' needs.

DBT-S and Relapse Prevention

Relapse Prevention (RP) was developed by Marlatt and Gordon (1985). This approach helps clients to identify high risk situations and triggers that might lead to a slip and to develop a cognitive-behavioral plan to address them. Like DBT-S, RP embraces Eastern philosophies around acceptance and balance.

DBT-S and RP strategies have significant overlap and are highly compatible. Therapists are encouraged to use these teachings and techniques in combination with this manual.

DBT-S, Twelve-step, and Traditional Alcohol and Drug Counseling

Twelve-step and traditional alcohol and drug counseling propose a disease model to explain SUDs. From these treatments' perspective, addiction has a progressive course that will eventually result in serious consequences or even death if complete abstinence is not achieved.

A important component of step-work and traditional alcohol and drug counseling is that clients enter treatment committed to abstinence, that they admit to being powerless over substances, and that they regularly attend meetings as the preferred method to maintain sobriety. Emphasis is placed on the importance of fellowship, working the steps, and on a relationship with a higher power. Resistance to the methods of these approaches is frequently characterized as denial and part of the disease process.

In contrast to these approaches, DBT-S focuses less on a disease model and more on how emotion dysregulation, invalidating environments, and skills deficits influence SUDs. DBT-S postulates that behavioral factors and environmental contingencies strongly influence and even control substance use. Through behavioral analysis and skills training, clients learn to respond effectively to cues for substance use, eventually making more sweeping behavioral changes over time.

However, the emphasis on behaviorism in DBT-S does not negate a disease model etiology. DBT theories (i.e., the biosocial model) provide for genetic and biological contributions to problems, and people with progressive diseases and behavioral difficulties both need to learn skills to manage these conditions. Those working the steps can also benefit from using skills when stress arises during that process.

Another contrast is the DBT-S view of abstinence in comparison to Twleve-step and traditional approaches. DBT-S, while also abstinence-based, does not require immediate abstinence to begin treatment and may not require total abstinence from substances for all clients (e.g., a client who quits drugs may still drink alcohol if it does not create functional problems, is not a contributing factor to other problem behaviors, and is not a dysfunctional coping behavior; admittedly, this situation likely represents the exception rather than the rule). DBT-S also accepts that clients often need to take psychotropic medications to address symptoms of mental illness.

Despite theoretical and philosophical differences, wise practitioners will seek a dialectical synthesis between the approaches[5]. The reality is that the vast majority of clients will end up using what works without struggles over ideological purity to one approach over another. Many successful programs, such as the Hazelden Model, have thoughtfully used Twelve-step work and cognitive-behavioral techniques in harmony with each other. Indeed, this manual incorporates some Twelve-step teachings and exercises imbedded in the skills presented.

The author encourages clients to attend various Twelve-step meetings when they may be a beneficial addition to their treatment (why not encourage clients to use as many resources as possible?), and clients tend to report that those meetings and the people they meet there bolster their recovery.

---

[5] Seeking sensible resolutions grounded in research evidence on disparate theories and approaches is the reason for the "Role of Contextualism in Applying DBT-S" section that follows.

DBT-S and Harm Reduction Practices ————————————

Harm reduction practices aim to reduce the adverse health, social, and economic consequences of alcohol and drugs without necessarily reducing consumption.

Harm reduction recognizes that many people who use alcohol and drugs may be unable or unwilling to decrease or quit use, so interventions and measures aimed at decreasing the negative effects of substance use for both individuals and society are needed. Practical and feasible measures vary based on the type of substance, the particular target population and community, and a complete assessment of specific risks and harms.

A common example of harm reduction on a societal level is providing clean needles to people who use intravenous drugs to minimize the spread of HIV and other blood-borne illnesses. However, harm reduction can take many forms including minimizing health impacts and decreasing the impacts of use on housing, employment, education, and relationships. The author's perspective is that harm reduction is helpful and should be applied on both large (societal) and small (individual) scales with the goal of keeping people as educated, healthy, and safe as possible.

Harm reduction, like DBT-S, advocates a non-judgmental, non-pejorative approach toward people who have substance use problems. Also similar to DBT-S, harm reduction recognizes small changes toward larger goals, knowing that keeping people as healthy as possible through minimizing the potential negative impacts of substance use represents a step toward eventual abstinence (even though harm reduction does not advocate for abstinence, perse).

DBT-S embraces harm reduction practices to minimize the deleterious effects of substance use when it occurs. Nonetheless, a key difference is that DBT-S does not waiver from promoting abstinence as a treatment goal. Dialectically, this means respecting and finding validity in two seemingly opposing positions at times.

Role of Contextualism in Applying DBT-S

While research demonstrates the efficaciousness of DBT-S as applied in Linehan's treatment framework (i.e., the standard model), it is important to know that broad-based research also supports adaptations of empirical models to community settings. In other words, adherence (i.e., how closely therapists stick to treatment manuals) to Linehan's treatment framework and manual is not a prerequisite for effective outcomes.

Six decades of psychotherapy outcome research has demonstrated that no treatment model has reliably shown superiority to other treatment models[6]; DBT and DBT-S are not exceptions. The finding that treatment models have equivalent efficacy, often referred to as the Dodo Bird Verdict, is virtually an empirical fact and occurs because treatment models share therapeutic factors (i.e., common factors) that account for the vast majority of change (Wampold, 2001; Duncan et al., 2010). Frank and Frank (1991) highlight examples of therapeutic factors shared by different treatment models:

- the treatment alliance

- belief and expectancy on the part of both client and therapist

- a cogent explanation of the client's difficulties

- the coherent application of techniques and interventions to remedy the difficulties

- opportunities for client to learn, practice, and enhance self-efficacy

Research is clear that specific "ingredients" of treatment account for little change and are effective only in the *context* of the therapeutic factors. For this reason, adherence to the specific ingredients of a treatment model is largely unimportant and, in fact, meta-analysis has show that its effect on outcomes is almost zero (Webb, 2010). That said, while adherence is relatively unimportant, applying an approach *coherently* is necessary and part of contextualism. When applying DBT-S, it is important to be fluid in the techniques and interventions, but to remember the supreme importance of staying planted in the fertile ground of therapeutic factors.

DBT-S can be expected to be effective when applied with allegiance (i.e., the therapist's belief in the approach) and consistency, and when customized to the needs of clients seen in unique settings. Customizing treatment approaches, in this case DBT-S, is at the heart of evidence-based practice.

Evidence-based practice is defined by the American Psychological Association (APA) as using clinical expertise to decide the applicability of research to clients based on their culture, characteristics, and preferences (APA, 2006). Recognizing the limited external validity of empirically-supported treatments derived from randomized clinical trials, this APA policy thoughtfully expands our practice by empowering therapists to consider how best to treat clients through dialectically balancing what we know from research with how that research may need to be adapted and customized to individual clients. Simply put, overly prescriptive and inflexible treatment applications may have limited generalizability to clinical settings, compromising client care (Kazdin, 2008).

Monitoring treatment and using that data to adjust the approach as needed is also central to evidence-based practice. Using data collected at regular intervals to inform treatment planning and interventions and to improve treatment outcomes is referred to as *practice-based* evidence.

Guided by evidence-based practice, therapists need to decide the best application of DBT-S (or any other approach) to their population in their setting. Deciding how to structure the treatment according to level of care needs and other factors is discussed later in the book.

---

[6] The author refer readers to *The Great Psychotherapy Debate* by Bruce Wampold for a complete discussion of the contextual model of therapy and to *The Heart and Soul of Change* by Duncan et al., for a complete discussion of what works in therapy.

Further, while the author stresses applying DBT-S coherently with a consistent thread from theory through intervention, from the beginning of therapy through the end of therapy, he also stresses avoiding the trappings of schoolism: blind allegiance to an approach that leads proponents to develop a false sense of superiority. This sense of superiority often puts adherence to the treatment ingredients and the treatment manual over determining the most effective applications based on clients' needs[7].

In conducting DBT-S, the author encourages being grounded and centered in the approach while also looking at how other theories and interventions can be dialectically synthesized when it benefits clients. As examples, motivational interviewing and relapse prevention techniques blend well with DBT-S, as does applying stages of change. In fact, SAMHSA's IDDT guidelines call for combining elements of what could be considered "stand-alone" therapy models.

Thus, in adopting a particular approach (like DBT-S), mental and chemical health providers should avoid the temptation of ideological purity. As summarized by Connors et al. (2001):

> Over the past 30 years, a series of clinical trial research studies have compared treatments from very different theories to see which one was superior to the others. This 'horse race' research design has not found a single specific treatment for substance abuse that consistently does better than all the others (p. 214-215).

This validation of the Dodo Bird Verdict guides us away from ideological purity and toward evidence-based practice: using clinical expertise to determine what combination of approaches and interventions work best based on data and feedback from particular clients in particular settings.

---

[7] Movements that (over)emphasize treatment fidelity (i.e., competence in the approach and adherence to the manual) have not established sufficient evidence to support fidelity mandates. For example, specific ingredients account for little change, and there are both no empirically-supported training and research dissemination models and no evidence that replicating researched models with fidelity would result in better community outcomes. It makes much more sense to track outcomes in community settings and use them for program improvement.

An Etiology of Mental Illness and Substance Use: Emotion Dysregulation and Invalidating Environments

Consistent with the contextual model, DBT-S rests on a theory that explains how clients develop mental illness and why clients sometimes cope with substance use. This theory is what drives the treatment philosophies and interventions.

Linehan (1993a) postulated that emotion dysregulation that transacted with invalidating environments was at the root of borderline personality disorder. Although Linehan has focused on populations with borderline personality disorder, this theory of emotion dysregulation has utility with other populations too, so long as it is plausible and convincing to them (i.e., consistent with the contextual model).

Emotion dysregulation consists of being emotionally sensitive, emotionally reactive, and having a slower return to baseline when emotions are activated. When people have frequent, intense, and prolonged emotions, these neural pathways get sensitized and may get activated in an automatic, default manner. This chronic state of hyper-arousal and reactivity has been referred to by researchers as a "kindling effect." Like a campfire that appears extinguished the next morning, the emotional "coals" actually remain warm to hot, ready to flare back up into a firestorm when something as small as a leaf blows across them. These states of elevated and prolonged emotions are difficult to tolerate, making it seem impossible to choose effective behaviors in their wake.

These painful emotions lead many people to escape and avoidance behaviors that may be reinforcing in the short-term but that cost them dearly in the long-term, continuing the cycle of emotional turmoil. The most serious escape behavior is a suicide attempt, but others including self-injury, substance use, eating disorder behaviors, gambling, over-spending, and countless others flourish too. *One challenge in treatment is making sure that clients do not exchange one escape and avoidance behavior for another.*

In terms of substance use, many people report that getting drunk or high is one way to deal with painful emotions. When aversive feelings are escaped and avoided, the use of the substance is reinforced, ultimately leading to addiction problems that "self-medicate" emotions. The medicating of emotions is only a temporary fix as chronic avoidance of emotions ultimately leads to the intensification of them, playing into the cycles of maladaptive behaviors.

Another problem related to emotion dysregulation is mood-congruent behavior. As Linehan has noted, "emotions love themselves," and they often pull us into behaviors that keep them activated and aroused. As examples, depressed people engage in depressive behaviors, anxious people engage in avoidance, and angry people act hostile toward others. Like other escape and avoidance behaviors, mood-congruent behaviors tend to be reinforced through the avoidance of what is perceived to be and/or what is in reality, aversive. The depressed person who shuts down avoids life's everyday challenges, the anxious person who dodges fears is spared the greater anxiety that comes from approaching them, and the angry person maintains a sense of power and control that masks vulnerability.

Related to substance use, many people have reported another type of mood-congruent behavior: when something makes you feel better it is self-reinforcing so you might keep doing it. As tolerance to the substance builds, more and more of it is needed to achieve the desired way of "feeling," and addiction becomes probable. When withdrawal, feeling physically lousy, and painful emotions seep (or rush) back in, using the substance is the predictable way of feeling better again, supporting the cycle of substance use.

When clients work to discontinue self-sabotaging ways of coping with affect, they often default to judging the emotions that have caused them problems in the first place, perhaps believing that calling emotions stupid or wrong will make them go away. In reality, judging emotions tends to be as counter-productive as escape and avoidance, leading emotions to intensify over time, further sensitizing them and creating a greater need for escape. The solution, though paradoxical to clients, is to be willing to accept and have a relationship with emotions (and ultimately urges) in order to move through them. Many Buddhist practitioners have noted that it is the willingness to relate to our suffering that ultimately ends it.

This theory of emotion dysregulation is practical in that it drives our treatment interventions. In other words, as therapists we want our interventions to be guided by the theory and to coherently flow from it. In DBT-S, validation of emotion will be a primary intervention as it almost always calms emotional intensity. Similarly, interventions that decrease emotional vulnerability, such as self-care, and skills to create positive emotions and to step out of mood-congruent emotions will be consistently taught, encouraged, and reinforced.

Lastly, we come back to the use of acceptance and non-judgment as a primary way of dealing with affect. Having a curious understanding of emotions and a willingness to listen to and have a relationship to them is healing, and DBT-S therapists teach and reinforce this approach whenever possible. Through relating to emotions, clients develop an understanding of maladaptive behaviors rather than simply asking them to stop therm.

Practically speaking, we teach clients mindfulness skills to be aware of and to accept emotions and urges as steps toward responsive, effective behaviors, emotion regulation skills to modulate and balance emotions, and distress tolerance skills to cope when life seems unbearable.

When clients learn emotion regulation they can soothe intense emotions in order to inhibit ineffective behaviors and refocus attention and action toward effective behaviors.

The next section discusses the effects of invalidation on emotions and suggestions for using validation in treatment.

Invalidating Environments and Validation in Treatment

Validation is communicating the non-judgmental acknowledgement and acceptance of one's own or another person's feelings, thoughts, and experience. In Rogerian terms, it is understanding the phenomenological nature of a person, really seeing life from his or her perspective, and "prizing" the person. Validation requires pausing to connect and be with experience in the moment, to find and communicate its truth. Almost always, validation decreases the intensity of emotions. By contrast, invalidation can be thought of as any interpersonal response that increases the intensity of emotions.

Linehan (1993a) and others (Koerner, 2012) have discussed the role of invalidating environments in maintaining and intensifying emotion dysregulation. While no environment is perfectly validating (nor should it be), environments that are consistently and chronically invalidating fuel emotional fires. The observation of interactions between people highlights that emotionality often invites invalidation and vice versa.

Some forms of invalidation are obvious, and their contribution to problems is obvious. Many people who were raised in and/or are currently in abusive and neglectful environments will struggle with mental illness and/or substance use. Similarly, actively sending the message that a person's experience is wrong, incorrect, or otherwise distorted leads a person over time to mistrust his own experience and, consequently, that individual does not learn how to self-validate. Without validation from self and others, self-judgments and painful emotions thrive.

Other forms of invalidation are more subtle. The passive failure to acknowledge a person's experience, purposefully or as an oversight, sends the message that feelings, thoughts, and behaviors are insignificant and do not matter, or that a situation is not "any big deal." Another subtle form of invalidation is expecting clients to do anything that is not in their behavioral repertoire.

It is difficult for clients to move on effectively when their experiences are not adequately recognized and expressed by others in a non-judgmental manner. One of the primary goals of treatment is to create an explicitly validating environment in which clients feel understood and valued. In interpersonal terms, validation is about providing a corrective interpersonal experience in which a person receives what has long been missing: understanding. In behavioral terms, it is about reinforcing a person for attending to experiences, often painful ones, that require attention before behavioral change can occur. It is also a safe way to expose clients to their feelings. In general therapy terms, validation is a primary intervention for building the therapeutic alliance.

In conducting DBT-S, therapists must remember to start with validation, knowing how difficult it is for clients to use skills when struggling with symptoms of mental illness and substance use. When clients acquire and practice skills, improvement is not a constant, and many setbacks are likely. Validation of how difficult it is to learn and use skills helps clients to tolerate the ups and downs that come with building a satisfying life and to learn from falling into symptomatic behaviors and/or relapse. Without this emphasis on validation, it is difficult for the client to continue to practice and master skills.

Linehan (1997) has established six progressive levels of validation, listed below:

- Being mindfully attentive and alert

- Reflecting what the clients says

- Acknowledging what the client says and what is communicated nonverbally

- Acknowledging how the client's phenomenological experience makes sense given his or her history

- Acknowledging how the client's phenomenological experience makes sense in the present moment

- Participating in a genuine connection with the client as a human, not as an expert or therapist

Validation requires active listening, and accurate, nonjudgmental acknowledgment of the client's experience. Not only does validation enable us to stay with the client in the moment, not get too far ahead or too far behind, but it is essential to open the client up to change-oriented interventions. However, it is important to know that validation is not a means to end (i.e., something done to get to an intervention), but a person-centered method of being in real contact with another. *Make sure the client feels understood before moving on to change or problem-solving.*

Validation is especially important because it speaks to one of the most important therapeutic factors: the treatment alliance.

Structuring the Treatment Environment

Treatment Framework

Not adequately structuring the treatment environment may be one of the largest mistakes a therapist can make with clients who have complex co-morbidity. As a rule of thumb, the more difficult the problems, the more important the structure becomes. Because DBT-S is designed for populations with severe problems, it is vital to make sure proper treatment structure is in place. While different treatment frameworks are discussed in this section, note that DBT-S can be done exclusively in individual therapy with clients who do not require a higher level of care (i.e., clients' safety is maintained and they are making reasonable progress without the need for added treatment components or intensity).

Dimeff and Linehan (2008) have structured DBT-S similarly to regular DBT with a few additional components. Linehan's treatment framework for standard DBT includes four primary treatment modes, each with particular functions. While readers are referred to Linehan's (1993a) original book for complete descriptions, a brief synopsis of the standard model and DBT-S modifications is made here.

DBT, and DBT-S by extension, are multi-modal with weekly individual therapy and weekly group skills training components, plus 24/7 phone coaching provided by the individual therapist and weekly consultation group for therapists. In DBT-S, Dimeff and Linehan also added a case management component, a monthly friends and family meeting, and pharmacology. Additionally, the skills training group was divided into two sections so that clients would get an hour group skills training and an hour of one-on-one skills training.

The function of individual therapy is to increase the motivation of clients to overcome obstacles and use skills to reach their clinical goals. Knowing that dedicating time to skills training in individual therapy with multi-problem individuals can be challenging, the skills training group functions to provide dedicated time to classroom-style skills acquisition. Phone coaching functions to aid in the generalization of skills and to repair the therapy alliance between sessions if needed. The consultation group functions to increase the motivation and effectiveness of therapists (Linehan, 1993a).

The added components in DBT-S also have particular functions. Case management was added to help clients use skills and solve practical problems in their natural environments. Friends and family meetings were added to help loved ones better understand the treatment and to increase helping responses in their relationships. Pharmacology was added to ease symptoms of withdrawal and to provide needed medication-based interventions (Dimeff and Linehan, 2008).

Linehan's standard models of DBT and DBT-S work, but they are also complicated and not easily integrated across settings and populations. These models also may not be the appropriate level of care for some populations. For these reasons, readers may choose to apply the methodologies of DBT-S in a different treatment framework that suits their populations and settings more effectively. As Linehan (1993a) has noted:

> These modes constitute a service delivery model...I use the term 'mode' to refer to the various treatment components that together make up DBT, as well as the manner of their delivery. *In principle, DBT can be applied in any treatment mode* (p.101).

For example, no a priori reason exists to say that a group-based treatment program thoughtfully connected with other service formats (e.g., individual therapy, psychiatric services, case management) cannot be designed to meet the functions of DBT-S. In our experience, many clients who attend DBT and DBT-S programs have had previous contact with mental and chemical health systems, and they often have existing individual therapists, case managers, medication prescribers, and other supports. Recognizing that the elements of a "team" often already exist, the authors have had success respecting continuity of care issues and bringing these invested team members to the table. Within group-based programs we have applied the philosophies, skills, and interventions of DBT and DBT-S while clients and therapists closely coordinate with other providers, representing a dialectical synthesis of helpful treatment components.

A group-based format adapts the individual mode of standard DBT into a dedicated group therapy time, while also keeping dedicated skills training time, consultation, and phone coaching (see separate section on our phone coaching recommendations). The inspiration for this adaptation comes from Linehan (1993a):

> Although I have not collected any empirical data on this question, it is conceivable that the individual DBT described above could be duplicated within a group therapy context. *In these cases, group DBT might supplement or replace the individual DBT component* (p. 104).

Our group-based format has been structured in the following manner, with three separate sections taking place each program day:

1. 50 minutes of skills training

This session is conducted similarly to Linehan's (1993b) skills training group. The curriculum is rolling, usually starting with the mindfulness module, then proceeding through the distress tolerance, emotion regulation, and interpersonal effectiveness modules in that order, revisiting the mindfulness module after the completion of each of these modules. Skills training homework is assigned and reviewed during this session, customizing the skills taught to each individual's treatment plan. In addition to the classic modules in Linehan's (1993b) manual and this manual, skills can also be taught from other sources (Pederson & Sidwell Pederson, 2012).

2. 50 minutes of group diary card review, in which clients present their cards, receive feedback and validation, and identify treatment targets for the third session

This session gives each client five to ten minutes to go over the diary card. Clients ask one another to write their cards up on a white board (keeping the group mindfully focused and requiring the use of interpersonal skills). Clients participate by validating difficulties, identifying and encouraging skill use, and modeling the use of skills among other ways. Clients with treatment targets on the hierarchy must take therapy time in the last session described below, although clients may also take therapy time for other reasons when there are no identifiable hierarchical targets.

3. 50 minutes of group therapy that is facilitated from a DBT orientation, complete with skills-based problem-solving

This final session is the adapted individual mode from Linehan's treatment framework. Clients take time for identified treatment targets, and the group therapy process serves to increase their motivation and to help them practice skills in an accepting and challenging environment. The therapy time uses DBT-oriented cognitive and behavioral interventions, including behavior chain analysis.

Based on level of care (LOC) issues, clients can attend this type of program anywhere from once weekly, to three times weekly (e.g., intensive outpatient LOC), all the way up to five days weekly (e.g., day treatment LOC).

Clients in this treatment framework maintain their existing individual therapist or a referral is made if needed. Individual therapists need not be DBT-oriented, and in our experience, the work going on between our DBT and DBT-S program clients and their individual therapists is compatible and helpful in concert with the goals of the program. Clients in our programs are referred to case management, medication management, and other services based on individual needs and level of care issues. Additionally, we have held monthly family and friend meetings for all of our DBT and DBT-S programs.

Linehan's standard model and the group format outlined above are just two of many possible models in which DBT-S can be applied. The key is to have a clear framework and structure from which to operate, knowing that "clear treatment framework" has been found to be a common factor in empirically-supported treatments for borderline personality disorder (Weinberg et al., 2011), and that structure is a primary solution to managing complex comorbidities (Koerner, 2012). Another key is to consider how multiple formats (or modes) can be applied. SAMSHA (2012) notes that making services available in multiple formats like individual, group, self-help, and family formats is an important part of IDDT.

As alluded to above, treatment frameworks must be designed to be responsive to level of care issues for the target population. Health Maintenance Organizations have established practice guidelines to evaluate and determine the appropriate level of care needed by clients. Important considerations include the clinical history (including the course of illness and past treatment effectiveness or lack thereof), current presenting problems and diagnosis, co-morbidities, psychosocial factors, and current progress in treatment. Also important is that there is no equally effective treatment available that is less intensive and/or occurs in a less restrictive setting.

In general, clients with more severe problems require more treatment contact, and clients who are referred to DBT-S programs typically have not made progress in lower levels of treatment intensity. If clients have significant co-morbidity with functional impairments across domains (e.g., work, school, social, family), they typically require a program that meets more than once weekly or that otherwise has two or more coordinated therapy contacts. If clients have significant co-morbidity and suicidality or other safety issues, they typically require an intensive outpatient level of care. This level of care is usually represented by a program that meets three or more times a week. Clients who cannot clearly commit to safety with regard to suicidality from session to session need an even higher level of care such as partial hospitalization or hospitalization. As treatment effectively progresses, the standard of care is to identify less intense and restrictive treatment options and to transition clients accordingly.

Implementing an effective treatment framework is only one part of structuring treatment. Setting up rules and expectations is discussed next.

Rules and Expectations

Clear rules and expectations establish the behavioral contingencies that are central to successful programs. DBT-S is based on creating a balance of validation and accountability. Clients cannot be held accountable to treatment if they do not know the expectations. Clear expectations help clients identify what they are working on, what behaviors are not acceptable, and create the type of containment that helps them feel safe and on track. Operating within structure is also a life skill as most natural settings are structured to varying degrees. As a rule, it is effective to practice in therapy what works in the world; too little structure does not work in treatment or in life.

Remember a time when you have been in a nebulous, unstructured situation without a clear idea about what you were supposed to be doing. Often these situations cause anxiety, fear, frustration, or other emotions that can be difficult to tolerate. Clients who already have emotion dysregulation and chaotic, unskillful behaviors need clarity in their environments in order to learn skills. Not being clear about what is expected is unfair and puts clients in needless distress, an iatrogenic treatment response.

When clients join the treatment program, think about informed consent as the first opportunity to begin structuring. Discuss the diagnosis, the treatment indicated, the expected course of treatment, the pros and cons of treatment, treatment alternatives, and treatment outcome data that support your treatment as well as any financial obligations, and the limits of confidentiality. Then discuss the particulars of your DBT-S program, including the required treatment components, when and where the appointments are, the attendance policy, and the rules of the program. The items in this paragraph are not meant to be exhaustive (or conclusive), but rather to underscore that there is a lot of discussion to be had in properly structured treatment. Have all important policies written down, validate that the amount of information can be overwhelming (but be matter-of-fact, not apologetic), and let clients know that questions and discussion are welcomed.

These initial conversations are good times to start talking about treatment as an active collaboration, requiring both of you at the table, working hard together in a therapeutic alliance to reach agreed-upon treatment goals and objectives. Research shows that early agreement on the goals and objectives of treatment underlies the therapeutic alliance and is predictive of positive outcomes. For hesitant clients, the full use of commitment strategies (discussed later) will be interspersed in orienting clients to the program.

A complete understanding of the undertaking ahead represents mutual agreements--a therapy contract. Once agreements are in place there is a clear architecture to what will transpire. These agreements, saying what you do, also create trust as you do what you say. For this reason, it is of the utmost importance that all parties stick to the rules and expectations.

Abandoning structure, altering rules (programmatically or individually), or failing to address broken agreements represents Therapy-Interfering behavior (TIB). Difficulties by either clients or therapists in following the treatment framework, rules, or expectations should be openly discussed in consultation and addressed at the earliest available opportunity.

While different program frameworks and other details and policies related to structure will be determined in individual settings, below are suggested rules for a DBT-S program:

- Members are expected to attend all scheduled sessions. All absences must be planned with therapists by phone or in person prior to the absence. Documentation of absences may be requested. Three consecutive absences without approval or failing to attend appointments as established by the attendance policy will be grounds for discharge. Discharged clients must wait three months before re-applying to the program.

- Members are accountable to the attendance policies and may be discharged for violation of these policies.

- Members are required to be respectful with words, feedback, and behaviors with all therapists, program members, and other people in and around the clinic. Disrespectful behavior may result in being asked to leave, chain analysis, a behavior contract, or discharge.

- Members are not to come to group under the influence of drugs or alcohol.

- Members are not allowed to use or share any medications, alcohol, or drugs with anyone who attends this treatment program. Using or sharing medications, alcohol, or drugs will be grounds for discharge.

- This program is skills-based. Members are not allowed to engage in unskillful behaviors together. This includes but is not limited to: use of any alcohol or drugs, self-injury, or any behavior that is or could be problematic for one or more of the members (e.g., gambling). Participation in unskillful behaviors with other members may be grounds for discharge.

- Members are not to engage in alcohol or drug use or SI/SIB/TIB behaviors when on premises or in the immediate vicinity (e.g., the parking lot). These behaviors on premises will be grounds for immediate discharge.

- Members are to maintain confidentiality. Group issues are not to be discussed outside of group or during break. Breaking confidentiality may be grounds for discharge.

- Members are expected to participate in skills teaching, to complete assignments, to present Diary Cards, and to give validation, support, and suggestions to peers.

- Members are expected to take time to problem-solve and practice skills whenever significant distress is reported.

- Members are expected to complete homework and change analyses as assigned.

- Members are encouraged to form friendships with others in group. However, members are expected to be clear about their personal boundaries and be respectful of others' personal boundaries.

- Romantic or intimate relationships are not allowed between group members.

- Friendships with others in group may not be private and must remain skillful.

- Members are not allowed to use alcohol, drugs, or engage in unskillful behaviors together.

- Members are not allowed to keep secrets regarding other group members' harmful behaviors.

- Members are encouraged to use other members for support outside of group. However, members are not obligated to be available to others outside of group. Again, members are expected to be clear about their boundaries and respectful of others' boundaries.

- Members may not call other members after they have been engaged in SI/SIB/TIB.

- Members are expected to attend all scheduled professional appointments and comply with prescribed medications.

- Members are expected to honor payment agreements for copays, deductibles, and uncovered services.

- Violation of group rules may result in consequences including homework, behavior change analysis, suspension, and/or discharge.

Treatment Hierarchy: Identifying Treatment Priorities

Clients with high co-morbidity and multiple problems often have a crisis-oriented approach to treatment. Without guidelines for "what to treat when," treatment can quickly become a crisis drop-in center rather than a planful process that helps clients acquire and practice new skills and behaviors. To address potential therapeutic chaos, Linehan (1993a) developed a treatment hierarchy that determines what treatment targets get addressed in what order. The treatment hierarchy represents another method for structuring sessions that aids both therapists and clients. For DBT-S, Dimeff and Linehan (2012) created an adapted treatment hierarchy to account for co-morbid substance use. Because the treatment hierarchy consists of intervention *guidelines*, and not absolutes, this manual makes minor adaptations to increase clarity and utility. Further, this manual adds two new targets to the hierarchy: Substance Use Behavior (SUB) and Recovery Interfering Behavior (RIB), explained below. Behaviors to target in treatment, in order of priority with explanations, are as follows:

1. Suicidal Ideation (SI)

Simply, clients at significant risk for suicide attempts need to establish safety and stability in this area when it exists. Careful assessment of risk is required for every client, including a behavioral analysis of risk factors, warning signs, and situations that trigger suicidal behaviors. All clients with safety issues require a written safety plan as a primary treatment goal. Clients at imminent risk of acting on suicide need to be hospitalized if a clear commitment to safety is not communicated.

2. Self-Injurious Behaviors (SIB) and Substance Use Behaviors (SUB)

Self-Injurious behaviors (SIB) and substance use behaviors (SUB) are targeted after SI. Dimeff and Linehan's

(2012) design ranks substance use as the highest quality-of-life interfering behavior (see below). SUB is listed alongside SIB on this hierarchy because it is a primary focus of DBT-S. Whether to address SIB versus SUB (if they are both present) depends on the relative seriousness of the respective target behaviors. Similarly, there may be situations in which you prioritize SIB and/or SUB on the same level as SI with the same intense level of intervention (e.g., self-injury or substance use that could cause an imminent medical crisis or puts someone at imminent risk for serious harm). Remember that the hierarchy gives guidelines but is not a substitute for clinical expertise.

3. Therapy-Interfering Behaviors (TIB) and Recovery Interfering Behaviors (RIB)

Therapy-Interfering behavior includes anything that clients *or therapists* do that disrupts treatment. Common examples include not showing up, being late, not completing the diary card, not doing homework, not participating in therapy, and being disrespectful in the treatment environment. Virtually anything that interferes with the therapy alliance can be considered TIB. These behaviors are addressed high on the hierarchy to keep treatment on track and effective. Do not wait for TIB patterns to emerge--address TIB behaviors on the first occurrence.

Recovery Interfering Behaviors (RIB) are a specific type of TIB that sets clients up for a relapse. Common examples of RIB include not doing self-care, harboring resentments, being dishonest (including lying by omission if it relates to recovery), fantasizing about use, and exposing oneself to high-risk people, places, situations, and things that are associated with use. Like other TIB, RIB must be addressed before a pattern takes hold.

4. Quality-of-life-Interfering Behaviors (QIB)

These behavioral targets include all types of frequent crisis behaviors often with the associated overuse of crisis services as well as behaviors that actively interfere with having a satisfying life. Self-sabotaging behaviors, interpersonal conflict, and behaviors that threaten housing, schooling, and employment fit within this broad category.

In addition to the treatment framework--rules and expectations, and treatment hierarchy--remember that structuring relates to seemingly smaller details like starting and ending on time and respecting the time limits established to accomplish different therapy tasks (e.g., mindfulness practice, review of homework, setting goals for each session, skills training, providing equivalent time for each member, "closing" each session). The use of diary cards, chain analysis, safety and substance use prevention plans, and the systematic assigning and review of homework also speak to the value of structure.

Use of Phone Coaching

The use of phone coaching is perhaps the most controversial and sometimes misunderstood DBT mode. Standard DBT, and DBT-S by extension, requires the individual therapist to provide phone coaching availability to clients 24 hours a day, 7 days a week. However, the therapist's availability is dialectically balanced with limits, meaning that expectations are established that keep clients from overusing phone coaching. If clients call too much or too often at inappropriate hours, the therapist will explore how this interferes with therapy. Similarly, if therapists do not observe limits with phone coaching, they are practicing unskillful limits or boundaries that are considered Therapy-Interfering behavior (TIB).

The primary function of phone coaching is to help clients generalize skills to their natural environments between sessions. To meet this function, coaching calls are intended to be brief and focused on skills-building. These calls are not intended to allow for venting or to be phone "therapy" or social chit-chat. Similar to how calling too much or too often at inappropriate hours is considered TIB, choosing to not focus on skills and attempting to meet other needs through this mode can be considered TIB. Like any other TIB, ineffective phone-coaching usually results in behavioral chain analysis.

Clients are expected to use phone coaching *before* participating in suicidal, self-injurious behavior, substance use, and other problem behaviors. Calling after acting on urges is also considered TIB, and DBT provides a clear contingency that phone coaching is not available for 24 hours following acting on a problem behavior so that those behaviors are not inadvertently reinforced. Like any contingency, this rule needs to be clear to clients.

While 24/7 phone coaching is a part of the standard model of DBT and DBT-S, it does not have to be a necessary component of effective DBT treatment. In fact, dialectical therapists find that there are both upsides and downsides to this level of availability.

Clients who do not have therapists with 24/7 availability can practice acceptance that many life problems do not have immediate support and solutions. These clients learn to rely on Distress Tolerance and other skills along with other people in their support networks. They also learn to access support proactively with the knowledge that there are times when phone coaching is not available.

Therapists who choose to set limits on their availability model effective self-care and limits. They also teach clients about individual differences with boundaries.

In addition to traditional phone coaching, therapists can consider how more modern and widely used forms of communication such as text messaging and email can be used to help generalize skills and follow-up on homework assignments.

Of course, phone coaching is not the only way to generalize skills. Therapists should also look to meet this function through homework and written skills application plans.

All therapists who provide phone coaching (whether it is 24/7 or following an adapted plan) need to establish phone coaching agreements up front so that everyone knows the rules and expectations. Below are suggested guidelines for phone coaching:

- Phone coaching is for the generalization of skills.

- Phone coaching must be used before acting on urges to hurt yourself or use substances.

- Phone coaching cannot be used for 24 hours after engaging in self-injury, substance use, or other Therapy-Interfering behavior (TIB).

- A phone coaching worksheet must be completed before the call.

- Phone coaching will focus on skills and not be therapy-oriented.

- Phone coaching will be limited to 3 to 5 minutes.

- Not respecting the specific availability and limits of phone coaching agreed to by you and your therapist will be treated as TIB.

In addition to these guidelines, it is strongly recommended that clients complete a phone coaching worksheet prior to a call. Completing a worksheet, like the sample that follows, orients clients toward problem-solving and skills work and away from unstructured ways of engaging with therapists. Clients who fill out a worksheet also solve a lot of their own problems without having to call their therapists, gaining an increased sense of self-efficacy in the process.

Phone Coaching Worksheet

Please complete this worksheet prior to calling for coaching.

Describe the problem or difficulty:

Describe the skills you have already used:

Describe what specific skills you need help with:

Describe what other skills or supports you can use if your therapist is not immediately available:

Specific Expectations:

The call will focus on skills and last no more than 5 minutes.

I will be willing to be coached and practice the specific skills.

I will be respectful of my therapist's availability and limits.

I understand that I will be hospitalized if I am unclear about safety issues.

Treatment Stages and Stages of Change

DBT-S emphasizes a stage-oriented approach to treatment, as does IDDT. Many practitioners also use Prochaska and DiClemente's stages of change model to guide clients through treatment. These three systems will be described including how they overlap conceptually with one another. All three systems have utility in the treatment of dual disorders and should be evaluated to best match treatment strategies to each client's situation.

Linehan's (1993a) treatment stages are as follows:

- **Pre-treatment:** In pre-treatment, the therapist works on establishing a commitment to treatment by establishing an alliance in which agreement is reached as to the goals of treatment and the methods for attaining those goals.

- **Stage one:** Stage one treatment is all about stability and gaining control over extremely problematic target behaviors, such as suicide, self-injury, substance use, Therapy-Interfering behaviors, and other behaviors that actively interfere with clients' quality-of-life. What to treat as primary in stage one is largely decided by using the treatment hierarchy. Behavioral control over these problem behaviors is accomplished through skills training.

- **Stage two:** This stage focuses on treating posttraumatic stress disorder, if diagnosed, along with assisting clients with experiencing emotions in a more complete and healthy manner.

- **Stage three:** Stage three addresses typical problems of living and having clients attain a life with ordinary ups and downs.

- **Stage four:** This stage exists to move clients toward more advanced goal attainment along with increasing freedom, connectedness, and joy.

IDDT stresses matching clients to these treatment stages:

- **Engagement:** In this stage, the client is not connected to treatment and there is no working alliance. The primary goal of engagement is developing rapport, sometimes through assistance with a practical need, such as filing out an application, dealing with an immediate crisis, or by giving general support. Directly addressing substance use is not a goal of engagement, although talking about mental illness and substance use issues will happen by the conclusion of engagement. The DBT-S pretreatment stage overlaps with engagement and the next stage, persuasion.

- **Persuasion:** In persuasion, the client now has a regular connection but is not yet ready to work on substance use issues and may not be ready to directly address symptoms of mental illness. The foremost objective of this stage is to build awareness that substance use and mental illness symptoms are problematic and interfere with life and to increase the client's desire to commit to treatment for both sets of symptoms.

- **Active treatment:** This stage is marked by a demonstrated desire to reduce substance use with clear progress, though not necessarily total abstinence. Active treatment seeks to build on success by further reducing substance use and encouraging abstinence along with increasing the effective management of the symptoms of mental illness. Stages one and two (and possibly three) of DBT-S correspond to the active treatment stage.

- **Relapse prevention:** This stage is identified by the client's being abstinent, or no longer suffering from the deleterious effects of substance use and managing symptoms of mental illness. At this point, treatment focuses on maintaining planful vigilance to avoid relapse with either set of symptoms and developing recovery in other areas, such as increasing function at home, socially, at work, or in school. DBT-S stages three and four best overlap with relapse prevention.

And the Transtheorectical Model of (TTM) stages of change used by many therapists include (Prochaska, Norcross, & CiClemente, 2006):

- **Precontemplation:** This stage is characterized by the client's not recognizing a problem, either related to mental illness or substance use. There is often no intention to change behavior at this stage. Interventions that fit well with precontemplation include developing the treatment alliance and providing generalized support and problem-solving, overlaping with DBT-S pretreatment and IDDT engagement stages.

- **Contemplation:** The contemplation stage is characterized by an increased awareness of substance use and mental illness issues along with some thought of taking action without an actual behavioral commitment to do so. This stage overlaps with DBT-S pretreatment and the IDDT persuasion stage.

- **Preparation:** During preparation, the client makes a clear intention to take action in the near future.

- Action: The action stage is reached when the client begins to demonstrate actual behavioral changes that are in service of reducing mental illness symptoms and substance use. This stage takes the most commitment and effort on the part of the client. DBT-S stages one and two (and possibly three) match the action stage, as does the IDDT active treatment stage.

- **Maintenance:** This stage is one of consolidating gains and working on preventing a relapse of mental health symptoms and/or substance use. This stage is also characterized by greater gains in functional improvements in important areas of life. DBT-S stages three and four overlap with this stage, as does the IDDT relapse prevention stage.

- **Termination:** In this aspirational stage, the problem behavior no longer has any threat of returning, and the change is permanent. While opinions differ as to whether true termination of an addiction can be achieved, anecdotal evidence suggests that it can.

The following table, expanded and adapted from Mueser et al. (2003), visually illustrates the interconnections among these treatment stage systems.

DBT Stages	IDDT Treatment Stages	Stages of Change
Pretreatment	Engagement	Precontemplation
	Persuasion	Contemplation
		Preparation
Stage One Stage Two	Active Treatment	Action
Stage Three Stage Four	Relapse Prevention	Maintenance Termination

These stage systems recognize that clients cannot move from where they are not. Understanding each client's readiness to engage in treatment and change will assist in matching interventions to where clients are in order to improve outcomes. It is useful to discuss how these stages relate to clients both with them in treatment and in consultation with other providers.

Refer to the next section on DBT-S commitment and orienting strategies for more information on how to engage clients in each of these stages.

Commitment and Orienting Strategies

Clients with dual disorders frequently struggle with commitments. Depending on stages of change, they may not want to engage in treatment, or they may be hesitant to try a new skill or behavior. When Linehan began her work with clients with borderline personality disorder, she noticed their resistance to change and developed a set of commitment strategies to engage them. Along with other techniques (e.g., validation, motivational interviewing) the following commitment strategies outlined by Linehan (1993a) can enlist clients to try treatment or simply a new behavior. These techniques can also be tailored to clients' particular stages of change.

- **Foot in the door.** This technique is used to have clients agree to something that virtually anyone would agree to in order to engage them. Examples include:

    □ A suicidal client might be asked, "Would you like to have a life where you didn't constantly want to kill yourself?"

    □ Someone struggling with drugs and resulting conflicts with friends and family might be asked, "Would you like to have more enjoyable and peaceful relationships with others?"

- **Door in the face.** The opposite of foot in the door, this technique asks for something or a level of commitment most people would reject. As examples:

    □ A therapist might ask, "Will you come to treatment on an indefinite basis until your problems are resolved?" If the client agrees, you have a large commitment. If not, follow up with a more reasonable request that will likely be accepted, such as "Will you try this program for four sessions, and then we can discuss what's working and what's not?"

    □ When presented with a list of skills, the therapist may request that the client practice all of them. If the client balks, the therapist would then request a smaller commitment, maybe trying two or three of them.

- **Tying to prior commitments.** This strategy capitalizes on the relative success of past commitments and accomplishments and relates them to the present moment:

    □ A therapist might say, "You recently had 11 days of sobriety. Can you agree to avoid alcohol until our next session on Monday?"

    □ If a client overcame difficult problems like homelessness and unemployment, she might be reminded, "Six months ago you managed to stay alive, somehow cope, and get out of that hole you were stuck in...how does what that took compare to what you may need to do now?"

- **Devil's advocate.** Playing devil's advocate means taking one side in order to get the client to consider, own, and commit to the other. Can work well when used with nuance:

    □ A therapist might say to an ambivalent client, "maybe it makes sense to continue using. Not having the responsibilities of relationships, a job, or having a home to maintain could have its advantages." If used accurately (i.e., the therapist knows the client desires those things and does not feel hopeless about obtaining them someday), the client will start to argue for decreasing or quitting use and will articulate the reasons to move toward those goals.

    □ If a client starts therapy over-enthusiastically, the therapist might ask, "are you sure you want to commit to the program? It might get hard and you might want to quit." In this instance, the client will hopefully fortify the commitment to treatment.

- **Freedom and choice in the absence of alternatives.** This technique emphasizes that "nothing but this (treatment, skill, choice, etc.)" is on the table, so are you willing to give it a go knowing that you are tired of the same old situation and options are scarce?"

Orienting techniques are another way to enlist commitment. Orienting is a traditional cognitive-behavioral technique that means describing how the therapy task at hand (e.g., obtaining commitment to treatment, explaining a skill, requesting a behavior change) will be of benefit to *clients'* goals (Koerner, 2012). What is vital with orienting is understanding what clients want and are striving toward, not simply defaulting to the therapist's assumption of what they want. For example, the goal of someone with a SUD may not be to cut down or quit use, but instead might be to play in a band, get a significant other, have a peaceful family life, or get a more fulfilling job. Astute therapists will suss out what is underneath and tie the commitment or the suggestion to that motivation or goal.

Dimeff and Linehan (2008) have also emphasized the "butterfly" attachment that comes with some clients with co-occurring disorders. These clients drop in and out of treatment, and just when the therapist thinks they have them, they fly away. Practitioners are encouraged to discuss this potential attachment issue when initiating therapy. If this issue applies, practitioners and therapists can discuss how to address it and how it relates to commitment to treatment and the treatment plan.

Because DBT is traditionally an action-oriented therapy, therapists need to consider the appropriate stage of change and not push clients too hard to change problems that rest in the precontemplation (engagement) and contemplation (persuasion) stages. Instead, therapists can lean more heavily on interventions that are better received in these stages, such as validation, rapport-building, symptom management, and solving practical problems. The subsequent agreement on initial goals can be reflected on the treatment plan.

Practically speaking, Dimeff and Linehan (2008) emphasize that it is important to consider increased client contact by phone, secure email, or by other outreach until the client is clearly connected to treatment. They also emphasize knowing where the client can be reached in the case of no-shows, and enlisting the support of family and friends with the client's consent. This information should be put into an action plan to use if the client appears to have dropped out.

Nonetheless, this author believes that practitioners need to be clear up front about the amount of client "tracking" and "chasing" that will happen (e.g., a limit can be made by clear attendance expectations and defining the point at which discharge from treatment happens). Practitioners being more committed and working harder than clients as a pattern is typically not effective; a dialectical balance is needed in these situations. Further, practitioners need to be careful not to reinforce a pattern where clients gain what appears to be more support for being out of treatment versus being in it[8].

In terms of therapeutic factors needed to engage clients, DeFife and Hilsenroth (2011) emphasize the importance of meeting clients with positive expectations, providing clear contingencies around the roles of clients and therapists, including who does what and what the content and course of treatment will look like, as well as collaborating on short- and long-term goals based on clients' concerns.

Following is an example of a commitment agreement form.

---

[8] One could argue that dropout behavior is maintained by the reinforcement that comes from escape (or another need met by using), and that the therapist's relationship is not reinforcing (and may even be unwelcome). While that may be the case with some clients, sacrificing the structure of your therapy or program to make ever-increasing efforts to pull a client in is a poor trade. As the author has said to a "butterfly" client, "I would chase you forever if I could, but the rules say that if you miss one more time I need to discharge you, and you need to trust that I say what I do and do what I say if I'm your therapist."

Commitment Agreement Form

The following information has been explained to me, with an opportunity to ask questions for clarification:

- My diagnosis

- My expected course of treatment

- My individualized treatment plan with initial goals

- The program and/or individual rules and expectations

- The program and/or individual attendance policy

- The cost and my financial responsibility (e.g., copays, deductibles, payment agreements)

- Other important information

I agree to make a good faith investment in the program and/or individual therapy with my willing participation for a period of _____ or _____ sessions. As a part of this commitment, I agree to follow the program and/or individual rules, expectations, and attendance policy. At the conclusion of this commitment period, my therapist(s) and I will evaluate the course of treatment and decide among the following options:

Continue the program and/or individual therapy with a new commitment agreement

Make an appropriate referral

Other arrangements

Signed by client: _____ **Date:** _____

Signed by therapist: _____ **Date:** _____

Original to client; copy to chart

Self-monitoring: Using the Diary Card

Clients use diary cards to track urges and target behaviors related to safety and substance use as well as to track symptoms, Therapy-Interfering behaviors, skills used, and other relevant issues. Self-monitoring with the diary card serves several purposes. It aids in building awareness, pattern recognition, and effective skill use, helping clients to generalize what is learned in therapy to their natural environments. It also structures the treatment environment and gives clients and therapists a wealth of important information about hierarchical treatment targets and other priorities for sessions.

Although diary cards can be customized, one used in the treatment of dual disorders should minimally track the following information:

- Suicidal Ideation (SI): urges and actions related to suicide as well as skills used to manage this area

- Self-Injurious Behaviors (SIB): urges and actions related to self-injury as well as skills used to manage this area

- Substance Use Behaviors (SUB): urges and actions related to substance use as well as skills used to manage this area

- Therapy-Interfering Behaviors (TIB): urges and actions related to undermining therapy as well as skills used to manage this area

- Recovery-Interfering Behaviors (RIB): urges and actions related to undermining recovery as well as skills used to manage this area

- Quality-of-life-Interfering Behaviors (QIB): urges and actions related to diminishing quality of life as well as skills used to manage this area

- Symptom levels of mental illness disorders (e.g., depression, anxiety, obsessions and compulsions, eating disorder symptoms, anger)

- Medication compliance

- Feelings

- Skill use under each category

- Progress on objectives

- Any other important information for an individual client to track

Be sure to explain and orient clients as to the importance of diary cards and how this self-monitoring will result in their obtaining their goals more successfully. Diary cards must be filled out mindfully on a daily basis, and clients should expect to spend 5 to 15 minutes a day to thoughtfully complete them. It is ideal to have them completed for the previous 24 hours at the same time each day.

If a client fails to fill out a diary card, does it at the last minute, or otherwise completes it without thoughtful intention, treat it as Therapy-Interfering Behavior.

The following pages have a sample diary card.

MI/CD Diary Card

	MEDS	SI	SIB	SUB	TIB	RIB	DEP	ANX	ANG	Other SX	Relax	Sleep	Self-care
MON													
Skills													
TUE													
Skills													
WED													
Skills													
THU													
Skills													
FRI													
Skills													
SAT													
Skills													
SUN													
Skills													

FEELINGS	POSITIVE EVENTS	Progress Toward Objectives
FEELINGS	POSITIVE EVENTS	Progress Toward Objectives
FEELINGS	POSITIVE EVENTS	Progress Toward Objectives
FEELINGS	POSITIVE EVENTS	Progress Toward Objectives
FEELINGS	POSITIVE EVENTS	Progress Toward Objectives
FEELINGS	POSITIVE EVENTS	Progress Toward Objectives
FEELINGS	POSITIVE EVENTS	Progress Toward Objectives

Role of Behavior Analysis to Create Change ———

Behavior analysis[9] is a technique used to understand what precedes and follows a behavior, usually called a problem behavior or target behavior. It should be noted, though, that behavior analysis can also be used to understand the application of effective behaviors, what helps to prompt them, and how the results of employing those behaviors differ from the consequences of target behavior (for this reason, the more generic term "action" is used in the sample behavior change analysis). When a sequential, step-by-step picture of the antecedents and consequences of any behavior is established, then the client can look at each step to problem-solve more effective skills or actions to use to create positive change. The overarching goal of behavioral analysis is skills learning, but the technique has other benefits too, such as exposing clients to painful emotions so that they can practice accepting and tolerating them.

Behavior analysis starts by identifying the specific target behavior. Examples might include drinking, self-injury, not participating in therapy, getting high, missing an appointment, not taking medications, or breaking a program rule. After the behavior is identified, the prompting event, or what triggered or set off the behavior is described. Then, it is necessary to investigate what made the client more vulnerable to acting on the target behavior. For example, did the client have poor sleep, miss medications, get into a fight, or leave open opportunities to use substances?

Once the target behavior, vulnerabilities, and the prompting event are well-defined, then begin to establish the links that bridge the prompting event to the target behavior. Potential links include emotions, thoughts, physical sensations, and other behaviors leading up to the target behavior. This step slows down the action so that the client can see everything that comes between a trigger and a behavior, building awareness of what is often missed unless explored in detail.

The last part of the behavior analysis is identifying the consequences of the target behavior. Consequences can involve the impact of the behavior on the client, on other people, and on the environment. It is also beneficial to see if certain consequences become vulnerabilities for future target behaviors. For example, if a consequence was feeling shame, then that feeling could make one vulnerable to escaping that painful affect through a target behavior like substance use.

With the sequence from vulnerabilities to consequences established, the client can then develop skills-based solutions for each step, starting with skills needed to reduce vulnerabilities and ending with skills for dealing effectively with the consequences, including making appropriate amends with others by repairing mistakes and correcting whatever harm was done.

As you conduct behavior analysis with clients (and teach them how to do it for themselves), orient them as to its purpose and how it will be beneficial to them. Also remember to be as specific and precise as possible, to be validating and encouraging, to maintain a non-judgmental frame, and to reinforce all efforts and accomplishments.

The following pages have a sample behavior change analysis. Also note that many of the worksheets in this manual follow the basics of behavior analysis: building awareness of what comes before and after particular behaviors in order to problem-solve with skills.

---

[9] Behavior analysis is often called chain analysis, or alternatively, change analysis.

Visual Behavior Change Analysis Directions

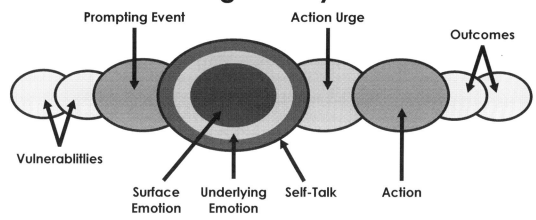

DIRECTIONS: The more you understand about behaviors you want to change, the more you can be effective in the use of your skills to meet that goal! Start anywhere on the change (chain) analysis and work forward and/or backward to figure out each link, then identify other skills or choices you could make with your new awareness. Remember to be NONJUDGMENTAL with yourself, the situation, and others. The following explains each identified link, but remember that you can add as many links as you need to understand your process and that EVERY LINK PRESENTS AN OPPORTUNITY FOR CHANGE! Also, look for skills that you might have already been using but not noticed or for which you need more practice. Chances are you have been using skills!

- **Vulnerabilities:** What made you vulnerable to the prompting event (and what unfolded after it)? Examples might include not doing self-care, having a tough day, getting into a conflict, or other stressors. Be as specific as possible.

- **Prompting Event:** What happened? Describe in nonjudgmental, descriptive words.

- **Surface Emotion:** What feeling(s) occurred after the prompting event that was/were most easily noticed?

- **Underlying Emotion:** Was there a feeling or feelings further below the surface? Examples might include feeling hurt or embarrassed under anger or feeling guilty under depression.

- **Self-Talk:** What automatic thoughts or beliefs were happening that fed your emotions and the following action urge?

- **Action Urge:** What did the feelings pull you to do? This link is a critical moment of choice in changing a behavior.

- **Action:** This is the behavior you might want to change. However, remember that using skills at earlier links might effectively change your action/behavior.

- **Outcomes:** What happened after the behavior you want to change? What did you gain and/or lose, in both the short term and the long term? Did the outcomes cause a new vulnerability or stressor and/or cycle back to the beginning again?

- **SOLUTIONS:** At each step, brainstorm skills or choices that could create behavior change and more effective outcomes. Also plan for how you can deal skillfully with the outcomes you are experiencing, including how you may need to make amends with others.

Visual Behavior Change Analysis Form

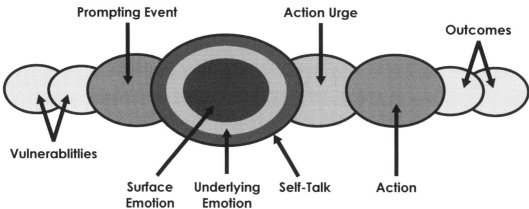

Describe your vulnerabilities:

Describe the prompting event (what set off the action?):

Describe your emotion on the surface (the one mostly easily noticed):

Describe any underlying emotions (the ones hidden underneath):

Describe your self-talk:

Describe the action urge:

Describe the action:

Describe the outcomes:

SOLUTIONS:

Fill in alternative skills and choices that would be more effective at each step. Consider how these alternatives would have altered the outcomes for you and for other people.

Describe how you will use skills effectively to deal with the outcomes that exist:

Describe who else was affected by your choice(s):

Describe how you will make amends with these people (if appropriate):

Skills Training: Philosophy and Approach

Clients who struggle with symptoms of mental illness and substance use often have skills deficits. It is not that these clients do not want to be more effective, but that they do not know *how* to be more effective. This is the value of skills training: clients need new behaviors to replace behaviors that have not worked effectively. Teaching new behaviors, so that there is something new to reinforce, is one of the most benevolent ways of promoting change.

The skills provide a common language for sets of behaviors that can be practiced to create a more satisfying life. As we teach the language and the concepts, it is important to be nonjudgmental about both the deficits and how the skills are taught.

As examples, many clients have learned that emotions are bad, so we teach a concept like "emotion mind" nonjudgmentally. Then clients can identify being in this state of mind without feeling blame or criticism: being in emotion mind just "is." Similarly, when a concept like effectiveness, or "doing what works," is presented nonjudgmentally, then you can ask if a given choice or course of action "is working" or if something else would be "more effective" without it being experienced as a critical, "gotcha" moment.

Virtually any situation is a skills teaching and learning moment. In individual therapy, skills will be interwoven in the approach. In a DBT-S program, there will be dedicated skills teaching time. Regardless of the level of care, the emphasis on continual skills training cannot be overemphasized.

As skills are taught, it is important to go beyond the intellectual understanding of skills to the experiential application. This involves considerable skills rehearsal and practice in individual and group treatment settings, followed by experiential practice in clients' naturalistic settings through homework.

In the teaching, application, and generalization of skills, it is important to continue problem-solving and refining of the skills, going from the course to the nuanced use of them. There is no finish line in the use of skills, only continued striving to be effective given the demands of each novel situation, with ongoing efforts to learn and implement skills more effectively.

Although this manual lays out the concepts and skills in a certain sequence, practitioners and clients may choose to alter the sequence based on what is most relevant and needed by a client or members of a treatment program. Meeting clients where they are with what is helpful and effective is the over-arching standard, not following a recipe. Keep in mind that the skills in this manual tend to be applicable to both mental illness and substance abuse (and life in general). It is up to the practitioner to decide how to "position" or "frame" skills, at times deviating from the text to customize to the client.

The skills and concepts in this book are not intended to be exhaustive. *It is important to supplement them with active discussion and information and exercises from other manuals and sources.* As Linehan (1993a) has noted regarding her skills manual:

> There is no a priori reason why one skills program cannot be substituted for another...what I am recommending is that if you do not use the DBT skills training manual as is, you consider either writing one of your own or modifying the manual to suit your own purposes" (Linehan, 1993a, p. 155)

Linehan's recommendation regarding her skills manual also applies to this one.

Excellent supplemental skills manuals include *The Expanded Dialectical Behavior Therapy Skills Training Manual: Practical DBT for Self-Help and Individual & Group Treatment Settings* (Pederson & Sidwell Pederson, 2012) and *Addiction Treatment Homework Planner* (Finley & Lenz, 2009).

Role of Consultation

Consultation group is an essential element of DBT and is a best practice for therapists of all orientations. In DBT-S, Dimeff and Linehan (2008) have referred to consultation as "therapy for the therapists." The stated function of consultation is to enhance the motivation and skill of therapists so that their clients can receive the best possible therapy.

Consultation follows DBT philosophies: it is non-judgmental, assumes we are all doing our best and need to do better, and is a dialectical balance of validation and change. Like DBT-S treatment, a 90-minute consultation group is structured with dedicated time for mindfulness (e.g., opening and closing with 5 minutes of practice), continued education and study of DBT (e.g., 20 minutes reviewing assigned readings and homework for therapists), and for supporting therapists in applying the approach coherently and effectively.

Similar to how clients have rules and expectations to follow, consultation group members must also follow agreements about attendance, preparation, participation, and taking a humble and dialectical approach to each other. In consultation, therapists regularly validate, challenge, suggest skills, and apply to each other the same strategies that are applied to clients: what's good for the goose is good for the gander.

Active, supportive, and accountable consultation groups reduce therapist burnout and build effective therapeutic responses, minimizing iatrogenic responses that undermine clients' treatment. Common examples of iatrogenic behaviors include lack of structure and accountability, extreme responses (e.g., too nurturing versus too strict), and causing or participating in boundary violations.

When evaluating how to respond to complex client issues in consultation, the authors recommend incorporating the following guidelines adapted from Beauchamp and Childress' (2001) and the American Psychological Association's (APA) basic principles of professional ethics:

1. **Beneficence:** Will what is suggested in consultation likely provide benefit to clients (or the therapist) and be helpful?

2. **Non-malfeasance:** Will what is suggested have a low risk for harm?

3. **Autonomy:** Will what is suggested respect clients' ability to choose and make decisions? Consistent with "consulting to the client," does the intervention and approach empower clients to use their skills and be their own agents in life?

4. **Fidelity:** Will what is suggested be true to the treatment agreements, including what was promised and the discussed rules and expectations?

5. **Justice:** Will what is proposed equitably balance the needs, rights, and resources of one client versus others in a group, program, or clinic?

These guidelines provide the consultative architecture for reaching ethical, effective, and balanced decisions regarding the care of clients and each other.

It could be argued that the consultation group is one of the most effective aspects of DBT since it directly benefits the therapeutic alliance. If you are unable to find or create a DBT consultation group, seek consultation from someone who values your clients and their outcomes over proving that their model or approach is better than yours (and show similar respect). In addition to scheduled consultation group, it is encouraged that you have a consultative milieu within your program and clinic in which therapists can consistently seek out support and guidance.

When to Refer

Clients need to be referred to a higher level of care when they fail to make progress in treatment in the timeframe in which reasonable gains are expected. Before referral, therapists should openly address barriers and make changes in the treatment plan if indicated. Revisiting rules, expectations, and agreements along with the use of commitment and orienting strategies may work, particularly if both clients and therapists are clear on the contingencies in play. In other words, defined behavioral benchmarks that specify if and when a client will stay in the current treatment versus being referred to a different option must be in place.

If there is a sudden increase in safety issues that put a client at imminent risk of suicide, homicide, or serious injury, or if there is a worsening of substance use issues to the point that the client displays little behavioral control, then a quick referral to a higher level of care with thoughtful transitioning is indicated.

Clients should always be hospitalized when imminent risk of suicide exists or when they are unable to clearly commit to safety and follow a safety plan.

Referrals to lower levels of care are made when clients have progressed to the point at which treatment can be effective in a less restrictive setting with less treatment intensity.

As a rule, remember that discharges to other levels of care should not be surprises, but based on contingent if X, then Y scenarios.

Part Two

SKILLS TRAINING AND WORKSHEETS FOR CLIENTS

Introduction to Skills Training

A hallmark of DBT-S is the explicit emphasis on learning and using new skills and behaviors to replace behaviors that are no longer effective, are unhealthy, and/or are unsafe. Unlike other approaches, DBT-S does not assume that people have the ability to change without new learning. In fact, it can be invalidating for others to expect you to change without assessing whether effective behaviors are in place to make it happen. Simply put, overcoming symptoms of mental illness and giving-up substance use is easier said than done and is not simply an issue of desire or "getting" and "staying" motivated. In DBT-S, we believe that a sense of motivation is accomplished by stringing together effective behaviors that are acknowledged, reinforced, and that work in getting you more of what you want and less of what you do not want. *The power of change comes through skills!*

In DBT-S, you will learn skills to:

- Manage painful emotions and crisis

- Manage harmful urges including urges to use substances

- Engage in healthy and enjoyable behaviors

- Regulate emotions

- Increase positive emotions

- Step out of behaviors that maintain negative emotions

- Set limits (boundaries) with others, say no, and ask for what you want or need

- Make and take care of relationships

- Create a more satisfying life

Learning skills requires some study and a lot of practice. After learning about some initial ideas and philosophies about dialectics and stages of change that will guide your recovery, you may be ready to start work on exercises that define your goals, your barriers to reaching them, and how to use skills to learn from mistakes and make progress. These exercises also include developing skill plans that include the *Suicide and Self-Injurious Behavior Prevention Plan*, the *Substance Use Behaviors Prevention Plan*, the *Mental Health Symptom Response Plan*, and ultimately the *Health Maintenance Plan*.

These exercises and plans are intended to get you thinking about and, most importantly, employing new behaviors. Start with the plan that addresses your greatest areas of difficulty as decided in collaboration with your therapist. Note that the intention is to get you going with the skillful behaviors that you already have in place. You will develop even more strategies as you progress through skills training.

As you work through each relevant plan, bear in mind that many substance use and mental illness symptoms are intertwined. Cross-reference and revise among the skill plans. You may ultimately choose to use the information from each plan to create your own customized integrated plan. Down the road, the *Health Maintenance Plan* will be the capstone when you have met most of your treatment goals and are maintaining your progress.

Creating a more satisfying life is a byproduct of effective action that generalizes to all aspects of your life. Keep mindfully practicing skills in your plans until they become a part of your behavioral repertoire and create lasting changes.

If you have this book, or if you are in a treatment program, it is a given that you have chosen to consider change, even if it is to please someone else. Your goals will vary depending on whether you are ready to embark on change now versus simply considering change. Even if you do not think you need to change anything, keep an open mind to DBT-S skills...*They are life skills that can apply to anyone, with or without problems, in any phase of life.*

What Are Dialectics?

Dialectics refer to a way of understanding and resolving the tensions that happen within us, between us, and in the world at large. A few basic assumptions make up dialectics:

- We experience opposing tensions, often perceived as contradictory. As noted above, these tensions can be internal or can happen between people and/or in situations. These dialectical conflicts, in which different positions arise, happen continuously. For example, many people in therapy experience the tension between doing what is familiar (staying the same) and doing something new (change).

- Each position in tension or conflict has its own truth or validity depending on the vantage point. There is no such thing as absolute or complete truth, and even the most contradictory ideas or forces have their own validity and are interrelated. No one position can exist without a relationship to another, with each part making up a larger whole. In the present example, there are valid reasons to stay the same and valid reasons to change, and all of those reasons are intertwined.

- Resolution of dialectical tensions or conflict occurs when one opposing force gradually or suddenly overcomes another, creating movement, change, a new synthesis, and ultimately a new dialectical tension. In this "stay the same versus change" example, each resolution point between the tensions leads to a movement of one type or another. Choosing to try something different, like using a skill, is an easily seen change. But even choosing to stay the same creates change too, though not always as easily seen. Doing what is familiar creates a new context that will lead to a new tension or conflict.

- Having all sorts of opposing tensions that lead to change is continual, and we make the most effective choices when we seek to understand the dialectic nature of our conflicts.

As you proceed through treatment, you may experience several common dialectical tensions:

Self-Acceptance versus Making Personal Changes

The inter-relatedness of these concepts is apparent. Self-acceptance is oftentimes the prerequisite to making personal changes (and is change itself). There are times and places for both.

Doing Your Best versus Needing To Do Better

At any given time you (and others) are doing the very best that you can with what you have. When you accept this assumption, you find compassion and self-acceptance. Yet doing your best is dialectically counter-balanced by the need to do better. That is the reason you are practicing skills to create a more satisfying life.

The next page has a list of frequent dialectical conflicts. Consider how each tension between these perceived opposites relates to your life (or the life of someone you know).

Frequent Dialectical Tensions

Following are common dialectical conflicts. See if any of these conflicts relate to you and brainstorm what approaches or skills could be helpful to resolve them effectively. Also think about and discuss other dialectical tensions that frequent your life and how to navigate them effectively.

Wanting to be different yet resisting change

Being pulled into versus stepping out of unskillful behaviors
(related to substance use and/or mental illness)

Wanting to use yet knowing it will be harmful

Seeing only one side to a situation

Being independent yet still needing help

Taking things personally when it isn't about you

Having a mismatch between your values and behaviors

Deciding a relapse means total failure

Wanting to be like others who don't struggle with substances

Feeling good in the moment with substances knowing it will lead to feeling lousy later

Deciding between a lie or the truth

Wanting respect but not practicing respect

Telling too much versus too little to others

Balancing your wants and needs with those of others

Separating feelings and facts

Staying non-judgmental in difficult situations

Leaving open options to act unskillfully

Taking an "all or nothing" approach to anything

Indulgence versus restriction

Balancing emotion with reason

Having your goals conflict with your current behaviors

Dialectical Abstinence

In DBT-S, dialectical abstinence means that you take the (undialectical) stance that alcohol and drug use is so destructive to your life that you commit to only to one side of the dialectic: working on sobriety. This one hundred percent commitment means that your sole focus is on learning and using skills to establish and maintain abstinence (Koerner, 2012).

It is a reality that many people who work on getting and staying sober have setbacks. If you make a mistake or have a slip, the goal is to remember dialectical abstinence and your 100% commitment to avoid a full-blown relapse. You do this by quickly repairing your mistake and throwing yourself completely back into your goal(s). What you want to avoid is giving up and working against yourself by making one mistake a bigger one, or worse yet, a series of bigger ones. If you were climbing a mountain and lost your footing, you would quickly re-stabilize, check your anchors, make necessary adjustments, and get back to climbing; you would not just throw yourself off!

As other analogies, successful people in any pursuit (e.g., parenting, business, sports) make mistakes, but the key difference between them and less successful people is that they actively learn from mistakes, sometimes mining their greatest opportunities from them. If a parent yelled at his child, the goal would be to learn and practice more skillful parenting, not to practice more yelling or escalate into extremely ineffective parenting. If a businessperson lost an account, she would learn and correct the mistake in the future, not commit the same error with her other accounts too. And if a pitcher gave up a home run, he would re-group and continue to try his best to get strikeouts, not just give up and start throwing slow, easily hittable pitches!

One hundred percent commitment to doing better flows from the skills of self-acceptance and being non-judgmental. Beating yourself up and getting into judgments is counter-productive to your goals and will not help you to do better. Remember the basic assumption that you are doing your best and need to do better, and resolve yourself to learn from mistakes. Use behavioral analysis with your therapist(s) and the philosophies promoted in this book to learn from relapses. This approach will improve your progress toward abstinence and a better life.

Note that the concept of dialectical abstinence can be used with other problems too, such as making a 100% commitment not to act on harmful thoughts such as suicide, self-injury, or substance use, and/or not to fall into behaviors that feed into symptoms of mental illness.

Stages of Change Descriptions and Worksheet ———

Change is continual, and we are continually changing. Change is also a process, and research has demonstrated that a process of change transcends all models of therapy and is at the heart of self-change efforts too. Regardless of where you are at in the stages of change, you are in the *process*. It is also noteworthy that you may be in different stages of change with different behaviors.

Each stage of change is listed below with a description of it. Based on these descriptions and other relevant information, discuss the stage that applies to you with your therapist(s) and fellow program members, as well as what might be helpful to move you to the next stage of your recovery.

Some general categories to guide you include information, support, supportive challenge, assistance in planning, problem-solving, and recognition of actions. Research has shown that people intuitively know a lot about what is needed to change, so tap into your intuitive knowledge to discover what will be useful.

From this discussion, record what will help in the space that follows the stage that best captures where you are at in recovery from mental health symptoms and/or substance use. When describing what you need, try to be as *specific* as possible.

Revisit this exercise throughout your treatment to determine where you are at in the change process and what you would benefit from at each step.

Precontemplation: In this stage people feel like they do not have problems aside from others bothering them about doing something different. People in this stage may also feel resigned and hopeless, perhaps thinking that the current state of affairs is their destiny.

What will help you most at this stage?

Contemplation: This stage is characterized by knowing that problems exist, but not being ready to do anything about it. Sometimes people can be in this stage for a long time. Knowing that change is a journey, many contemplators do not yet feel up to the journey.

What will help you most at this stage?

Preparation: At the transition from contemplation to preparation, the focus on solutions and the future start to solidify. Because doubts about change often still exist during preparation, it is beneficial to make intentions to change public to bolster resolve. Chances of long-term success are improved by careful assessment and planning and not rushing too fast into action. Any journey requires careful preparation to go the distance.

What will help you most at this stage?

Action: This stage is most easily identified as change (although all of the stages are equally important in the process of change). During action people are actively moving down the road toward the destination, whether that means sobriety or overcoming the symptoms of mental illness. During this stage you will be actively learning, practicing, and using skills to tackle specific issues and to create a better life.

What will help you most at this stage?

Maintenance: This stage is a time when people work to reinforce their accomplishments and to prevent lapses into old behavior. Maintenance is an active process that requires ongoing attention to the continuation of new behaviors and skills while avoiding and planning for the pitfalls that accompany the reappearance or threatened reappearance of old behaviors.

What will help you most at this stage?

Termination: Some people ultimately reach a place in which the temptations, urges, and difficulties that could trigger a setback no longer have any hold over them. Other people stay in maintenance for the long-term: both stages represent the culmination of great efforts in realizing change.

Dialectical Discrepancies and Stages of Change Worksheet

We often have behaviors that actively work against and sabotage what we want in life. This exercise starts with two lists. In the first column, list what you would like in each major life area. In the second column, list the current problem behaviors that create barriers to realizing your life goals. Then consider how ready you are to address each area based on the Stages of Change.

The last part of this exercise involves detailed behavior analysis around difficult behaviors to determine the vulnerabilities and triggers that lead to the behavior as well as the consequences of the behaviors. With increased awareness, problem-solving with skills can be applied to each part of the analysis.

Once you are committed to trying to tackle a problem behavior with skills, consider "going public" with your intention to take steps toward a better life.

My Life Goals   ## Behaviors that Create Barriers

Mental Health

List the Stage of Change that applies to addressing this area:

Physical Health

List the Stage of Change that applies to addressing this area:

Spiritual Health

List the Stage of Change that applies to addressing this area:

Family

List the Stage of Change that applies to addressing this area:

Friends

List the Stage of Change that applies to addressing this area:

Education/Self-Learning

List the Stage of Change that applies to addressing this area:

Work/Volunteering/Productivity

List the Stage of Change that applies to addressing this area:

Leisure

List the Stage of Change that applies to addressing this area:

Pick one area and do problem-solving. You may start with an area and problem behaviors that you think you are most ready to address based on the Stages of Change. In time, you will complete this exercise for each area.

Describe in more detail what makes you vulnerable to doing these problem behaviors and how they are specifically triggered:

Describe in more detail the consequences of these problem behaviors and exactly how they interfere with your life goals in this area:

Describe in more detail the skills that can be used to. . .
Address your vulnerabilities to doing the problem behaviors:

Address your triggers for the problem behaviors:

Address the consequences of the problem behaviors:

Effectively replace the problem behaviors:

Describe specifically what you are committed to do to take action:

List the people you will share this commitment with today:

Remember that changing problem behaviors is a process, and stay focused on the life goals that you want. Each small step forward is a success, and each step backward is an opportunity to learn. Use these learning opportunities to teach you how to be more successful in the upcoming attempt, and keep stepping! How to do this is explained in the next section.

Setbacks and Change: What It Means

Many people feel demoralized by setbacks, slips, or relapses. Often these occurrences reinforce a sense of being powerless or hopeless. Thankfully, the evidence shows that setbacks are simply a part of change, and not a hindrance to it! People who successfully change problem behaviors have starts and stops, ups and downs, and they sometimes revisit earlier stages of change after a relapse.

The excellent book *Changing for Good* (Prochaska, Norcross, & DiClemente, 1994) has a wonderful metaphor for the process of change. The authors state that changing behavior is like climbing the Leaning Tower of Pisa. As you climb the tower there are times when you are clearly rising up, but when you circle back to the leaning direction it seems like you are going back down, at least until you circle back up. Overall, you are making progress up the tower, especially if you seek to learn from the "down" times.

This book sometimes uses words like setback and relapse, but the change authors noted above like to use the word "recycle" to emphasize that we learn from all efforts toward change. Each effort toward change has its lessons that can be used for the next attempt and, like recycling, the material of what was is transformed into something new.

Conscientious people do not judge their recyclables to be useless and throw them in the garbage. Instead, they make sure their recyclables make it to the recycling center. Treatment is your recycling center when steps forward are interrupted by a step back.

Make your mistakes useful. As Albert Einstein said, "Anyone who has never made a mistake has never tried anything new."

Along these lines, if you fall back, remember the acronym SLIP. In DBT-S, SLIP[10] stands for:

Skills

Learning

Improves

Progress

The following exercise will put this concept into action.

---

[10] In other substance use treatments SLIP has stood for "Sobriety Loses Its Priority." This definition implies a loss of motivation or desire to do well and seems inherently judgmental. The author has redefined this acronym to better fit DBT-S philosophies and to emphasize learning.

Skills Learning Improves Progress **Worksheet** ————

What made you vulnerable to the SLIP?

What triggered the SLIP?

What were the consequences of the SLIP (for both you and others)?

What did you learn from the SLIP?

What skills can you use to avoid a similar SLIP?

What skills can you use to deal with the consequences (so they do not become vulnerabilities)?

What skills can you use to make amends with yourself?

What skills can you use to make amends with others?

What are you committed to do to move forward?

With whom are you going to share this commitment?

Suicide and Self-Injurious Behavior Prevention Plan

Complete this plan as a primary goal of treatment to build awareness about your suicidal and/or self-injurious patterns and to develop alternatives to them. As you learn more skills, revise the plan, and remember to review it daily and to practice it.

List the reasons why you want to work on eliminating suicidal and self-injurious behaviors:

List the short- and long-term consequences that often follow suicidal and/or self-injurious behaviors and/or how these behaviors interfere with your goals and life:

List your strengths and resources to avoid suicidal and self-injurious behaviors including skills and behaviors that have helped in the past:

List what makes you vulnerable to suicidal and/or self-injurious behaviors (e.g., consider feelings, thoughts, behaviors, what is or is not happening in relationships and your environment, self-care issues, etc.):

List the skills and behaviors you can use to decrease your vulnerability to suicidal and/or self-injurious behaviors:

List the warning signs that often lead to suicidal and/or self-injurious behaviors (i.e., indications that you are in the danger zone):

List the skills and behaviors you can use to respond effectively to your warning signs:

List primary triggers that immediately precede and "set off" suicidal and/or self-injurious behaviors (e.g., consider feelings, thoughts, behaviors, what is or is not happening in relationships and your environment, self-care issues, etc.):

List the skills and behaviors you can use effectively to remove and/or respond to your primary triggers and urges:

List ways you can burn the bridge between your urges and reacting with suicidal and/or self-injurious behaviors:

List the self-care skills and behaviors that decrease your overall vulnerability and that are important to use at all times:

List the skills and behaviors to replace suicidal and/or self-injurious behaviors and to tolerate distress and/or crisis:

List the people in your personal support system, their contact information, and their availability:

List the people in your professional support system, their contact information, and their availability:

If you are unable to maintain your safety with suicidal behaviors, call 911 or go to the hospital for assistance.

Substance Use Behavior Prevention Plan ——————

Complete this plan as a primary goal of treatment to build awareness about your substance use patterns and to develop alternatives to substance use. As you learn more skills, revise the plan, remember to review it daily, and practice it. If you have a SLIP (Skills Learning Improves Progress), use that situation to revise and add to this plan.

List the reasons why you want to work on decreasing substance use and/or achieving and maintaining abstinence:

List the short- and long-term consequences that often follow substance use and/or how substance use interferes with your goals and life:

List your strengths and resources for decreasing use and/or achieving and maintaining abstinence, including skills and behaviors that have helped in the past:

List what makes you vulnerable to substance use (e.g., consider feelings, thoughts, behaviors, what is or is not happening in relationships and your environment, self-care issues):

List the skills and behaviors you can employ to decrease your vulnerability to use substances:

List the warning signs that often lead to substance use (i.e., indications that you are in the danger zone):

List the skills and behaviors you can use to effectively respond to your warning signs:

List primary triggers that immediately precede and "set off" substance use urges and/or substance use itself (e.g., consider feelings, thoughts, behaviors, what is or is not happening in relationships and your environment, self-care issues):

List the skills and behaviors you can use to effectively remove and/or respond to your primary triggers and urges:

List ways you can burn the bridge between your urges and reacting with substance use:

List the self-care skills and behaviors that decrease your overall vulnerability and that are important to use at all times:

List skills and behaviors to replace substance use and to tolerate distress and/or crisis:

List the people in your personal support system, their contact information, and their availability:

List the people in your professional support system, their contact information, and their availability:

If you have a SLIP, describe your action plan for minimizing the mistake, repairing it, and getting back to your goal of decreasing substance use and/or achieving and maintaining abstinence:

Mental Health Symptoms Response Plan ——————

Complete this plan as a primary goal of treatment to build awareness about your symptom patterns and to develop effective ways of managing them. As you learn more skills, revise the plan, remember to review it daily, and practice it.

List the reasons why you want to work on decreasing and managing your symptoms of mental illness:

List your diagnosis and the symptoms you experience:

List the short- and long-term consequences of your symptoms not being actively managed and how these symptoms interfere with your goals and your life:

List your strengths and resources for decreasing and managing your symptoms, including skills and behaviors that have helped in the past:

List the vulnerabilities that might lead to a worsening of your symptoms (e.g., consider feelings, thoughts, behaviors, what is or is not happening in relationships and your environment, self-care issues):

List the warning signs that your symptoms might worsen:

List the skills and behaviors you can use to respond effectively to your warning signs:

List primary triggers that immediately precede and "set off" an increase in symptoms (e.g., consider feelings, thoughts, behaviors, what is or is not happening in relationships and your environment, self-care issues):

List the skills and behaviors you can use effectively to remove and/or respond to your primary triggers and urges:

List the self-care skills and behaviors that decrease your overall vulnerability and that are important to use at all times:

List the skills and behaviors to decrease and manage your symptoms and tolerate distress and/or crisis:

List the people in your personal support system, their contact information, and their availability:

List the people in your professional support system, their contact information, and their availability:

Health Maintenance Plan

Complete this plan when you have entered the maintenance stage of recovery with substance use and mental illness symptoms.

Describe how maintaining abstinence and managing mental health symptoms has improved your life:

List the self-care skills that you continue to use daily to maintain your recovery:

Describe the vulnerabilities and triggers that could lead to a relapse of substance use and/or mental illness symptoms:

List the primary skills and behaviors that you use daily to maintain your recovery:

List the secondary skills and behaviors that you use daily to maintain your recovery:

List the personal and professional supports you use to maintain your recovery:

Mindfulness Module

Mindfulness has been around since the dawn of humankind. The essence of mindfulness is the ability to collect and focus our attention, to sustain our concentration and to make responsive choices in how to direct our mental processes and subsequent behavior. To be responsive, we need to be awake and connected to each here-and-now moment.

The pursuit of mindfulness is like the pursuit of physical fitness: There is no finish line or terminal goal to reach. Instead, the daily practice of mental and physical fitness is worthwhile in and of itself in order to be as healthy as possible. Research continues to show that mindfulness practice has lasting positive effects both in terms of brain neurochemistry and in overall health.

Many of us suffer from what could be called an "untrained" mind. Like a body that has not been systematically exercised, an untrained mind does not perform well. It falls victim, often without awareness, to intense emotions and urges and to the never-ending barrage of stimulation that is encountered daily. This type of unquiet mind creates stress that is expressed both mentally and physically, and the deficits in sustaining and directing attention and concentration in the service of making responsive choices leads to a reactive lifestyle.

Just as physical exercise leads to optimal physical performance and relaxes the body, mindfulness exercise creates optimal mental performance and ultimately relaxes and quiets the mind, leading to peace, serenity, and more responsive living.

DBT-S has specific states of mind and core mindfulness skills to practice daily to train the mind and be more effective in life. This section will also cover awareness of emotional cycles, substance use cycles, and triggers for substance use.

As you practice the skills in the mindfulness module, remember the words of a famous Koan:

Before enlightenment, chop wood and carry water;
after enlightenment, chop wood and carry water.

States of Mind

DBT-S identifies three basic states of mind: "Emotion Mind," "Reason Mind," and "Wise Mind." As seen in the diagram below, Wise Mind is the dialectic balance between emotion and reason.

Emotion   **Reason**

None of the states of mind are good or bad, or right or wrong. Instead of judging states of mind, we simply consider if a given state is helpful or works in a given situation, or if a shift to another spot on the continuum would be more effective.

For example, being in emotion mind can be quite effective sometimes, in particular if you need to be motivated into action quickly. Think about how a spike in fear motivates a parent to run after a child who has wandered into the street. Because emotions have the adaptive function of organizing and motivating behavior, some degree of emotion is inherently useful in most situations.

That said, emotion mind can be a difficult place to be stuck, especially when emotions and urges seem overwhelming and never-ending. Seeing just from emotion mind often leads us to try to escape and avoid discomfort through rejecting and invalidating emotions and getting into unhealthy coping behaviors such as self-harm and substance use. In addition to escape and avoidance behaviors, emotion mind can lead to mood-congruent behaviors; these type of behaviors typically feed emotions and continue to create the same unwanted emotions over and over again. Examples of mood-congruent behaviors include isolating when depressed, avoiding when anxious, and getting into hostile or passive-aggressive behaviors when angry.

Like emotion mind, reason mind can be effective too. Occasionally there are problems that require a purely logical response. As examples, creating a budget on a fixed income may require reason mind, or working through a protocol during an emergency may require reason mind.

However, reason mind also has its pitfalls. Being stuck in reason mind can lead to the neglect of emotions, which can result in intensifying them over time. An example includes intellectualizing, a thinking behavior where excessive reasoning leads one to avoid uncomfortable emotional experiences. Like escape and avoidance through substance use or other behaviors, ignoring emotions through maintaining a purely "logical" position tends to be self-defeating. Staying only in reason mind also means that we cannot benefit from the adaptive information and motivations that come from emotions.

In most situations, we are most effective in Wise Mind. In this state of mind we are awake and connected to emotions along with our ability to reason. Effective action springs responsively from a centered and balanced place, even when strong emotions and urges exist. Wise Mind is both intuitive and thoughtful, and being an expression of the true self, the behaviors we choose from this state of mind reflect true values and intentions.

Clear Mind

For people who struggle with substance use, three additional states of mind can be helpful to guide recovery. These states of mind include "Addiction Mind," "Clean Mind, "and "Clear Mind."

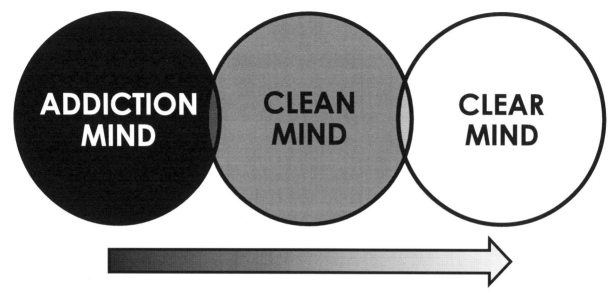

When people are still using or are in the early stages of change, they are frequently stuck in what can be called addiction mind. This state of mind is focused on urges and cravings to use along with alcohol- and drug-seeking and planning behaviors. Addiction mind keeps the doors to use wide open. In addiction mind, a myopic view of use keeps people from seeing the consequences of continued use. They are ready and willing to deceive both themselves and others in the pursuit of substance use. From traditional treatment approaches, being in addiction mind is similar to being caught in denial or ambivalence about giving up substances.

Once people have obtained sobriety through treatment or other means, they can then be stuck in what is called clean mind. One example of this state of mind is a "treatment high" in which the person moves quickly forward but neglects underlying issues, making a relapse more likely. Clean mind is also characterized by being naive to warning signs, triggers, and environmental cues to substance use and not being sufficiently proactive and planful to avoid relapse. In clean mind, people may also fall into the trap of believing that they have enough behavioral control to go back to "moderate" use.

As with Wise Mind, ultimately we want to move into Clear Mind. From traditional treatment approaches, Clear Mind is similar to being in the responsive state of sustained recovery. In Clear Mind, strong emotions and urges are non-judgmentally acknowledged and respected, and people are proactive and planful about how to handle them. Clear Mind has no illusions about how falling into old behaviors and relapsing can occur subtly and outside of awareness without sufficient practice of mindfulness, self-care, and use of resources. *The path to Clear Mind comes from decreasing use, achieving abstinence, managing physical and psychological discomfort, dealing effectively with urges, and keeping doors to use closed while working on skills to build a satisfying life.* In Clear Mind, the continued practice of effective behaviors happens moment by moment, one day at a time, even after many years of abstinence.

Two Steps to Wise Mind/Clear Mind

The following two steps give us ability to get into Wise Mind and Clear Mind.

Step One: Observe and describe, non-judgmentally and one-mindfully

Observing and describing is a process of waking-up, being aware of experience, and allowing it to flow. We begin by collecting and unifying our attention and then focusing our concentration. Think about having different mental windows: windows to emotions, windows to urges, windows to physical sensations, windows to behaviors, windows to others and our surroundings, and windows to our senses. Of course, there are other windows too, such as windows to the past (e.g., memories) and windows to the future (e.g., planning). As we become aware and notice experience, whatever it may be, we then decide which windows to open and which to close, based on what is explained in Step Two below. As we look through our chosen mental window, we watch without clinging to or pushing away, because of either attraction or aversion. In other words, the experience is the experience, no more, no less.

The process of observing and describing is intended to be non-judgmental. While judgments can be useful on occasion (e.g., when we simply need to categorize information and move on, in a dispassionate manner), most of the time they cloud experience, either amplifying or diminishing "what is." The truth about judgments is that they are all relative; what is "good" or "bad" depends on the context of the moment in relationship to other moments. Problems are opportunities and opportunities are problems, for example. Judgments usually reduce perspective, like looking at the world through drinking straws. Think about times in which you attached labels to what was being experienced. Chances are something important was missed, and the negative labels probably added suffering to experience and stopped the flow of observation, leading to being stuck. When we are stuck, it is difficult to participate effectively in experience.

Our goal is to describe what we observe in non-judgmental language, again not adding to or subtracting from experience. This neutral way of describing uses factual language that is objective, without coloring the experience. In other words, this process of observing and describing is taking in information and reporting it in a "matter-of-fact" manner.

Observe and describe is meant to be a one-mindful process, again, in relation to what is described in Step Two. Linehan (1993b) used the metaphor "be like a guard at the palace gate" in explaining observe. Guards decide what to let in, what to let out, and they maintain a watchful focus. Similarly, we direct the focus of our attention and concentration with one-mindfulness, gently noticing and letting go of distractions, gently closing windows that blow open.

Step Two: Participate Effectively

Observing and describing creates awareness. When we are not awake to the moments of our lives, we live reactively. Reactive living leads to exacerbation of symptoms and substance use through escape and avoidance and/or mood-congruent behaviors. Once we are aware we have behavioral choice, and we can choose to participate in symptoms and/or substance use, or we can choose to participate in skills and behaviors that would be representative of Wise Mind and Clear Mind.

We decide how to participate based on what would be effective, or what "works." Effective participation means removing barriers, from yourself and/or your environment, in order to meet your goals and live your life based on your true intentions and values. All things being equal, how do you best play your cards, meeting the demands of the present situation? How do you move from point A to point B being responsive instead of reactive? *What are you willing to do to have a better life?*

Making skillful choices that work is one part of effective participation. The other part is experiential, connecting and being with experience. Being with experience means getting off the sidelines and into the game, going from reading the lines to playing the part, and moving from sleepwalking through life to living it, moment by moment, starting with this one.

The more you practice the skills and behaviors that are important to creating the life you want, the more you will find those skills and behaviors springing intuitively from Wise Mind and Clear Mind, because they will become a part of you.

Remember the Koan quoted in the introduction to mindfulness, and continue to practice the foundational skills used in these steps. Chop wood, carry water.

Nonjudgmental Stance (NJS), Self-Acceptance, and Change

No one has ever overcome the symptoms of mental illness and substance use through the judgments of self or others. In fact, harsh judgments serve to amplify problems and guarantee that people stay stuck in ineffective cycles and patterns. Judgments get in the way of change.

While judgments occasionally have functions, most of the time they skew the way we perceive reality, shutting us down from continued evaluation of the facts, and keeping us in a state of elevated emotions and stress. In judgment mind, we default into our reactive and ineffective ways of dealing with life without a real connection of our greater goals and values.

Staying non-judgmental does not mean evading accountability for choices. It is important to take responsibility for mistakes and falling into old patterns. Staying non-judgmental means that as soon as you have a SLIP (Skills Learning Improves Progress) into substance use and/or into symptoms of mental illness, you quickly move to learn from it and make the necessary changes in a matter-of-fact manner, avoiding self-criticism that becomes a vulnerability to engaging in ineffective behavior. A nonjudgmental approach helps you to dialectically create a "positive" out of a "negative".

A nonjudgmental stance is a prerequisite to learning self-acceptance. Self-acceptance means acknowledging, without judgment, who you are in this very moment, with all of your faults and shortcomings. When you accept yourself, you free yourself of struggling with your reality self. Self-acceptance is not resignation, but a process that releases your psychological resources toward the possibility of change.

Acceptance is both the catalyst of change, and change itself.

One Moment at a Time

An old adage in chemical dependency treatment is that someone may not know how to be sober for a year (or longer), but that person does know how to stay sober for a day (or shorter).

Whether working on abstinence or simply trying to tolerate something painful, time and progress are more manageable when it is taken in smaller chunks, one moment at a time.

Take whatever you are trying to commit to and put it into a manageable timeframe. When that timeframe expires, commit to the next manageable timeframe. Over time, you will link these smaller successes into sustained success. For example:

- On a difficult day, commit to not drinking or using drugs for one hour (or less) at a time

- Table the option to attempt suicide or act on self-injurious urges between professional appointments

- Commit to practicing skills in ten-minute increments

- Decide to wait on confronting someone (if you cannot be skillful) until the next day

- Make a commitment to treatment one week at a time

As you look to manage symptoms and urges within smaller timeframes, keep practicing other skills and throwing yourself into the behaviors that will create the life you want: one moment at a time works best when you are not "watching the clock"!

Observing and Describing Emotions, Thoughts, and Situations that Trigger Substance Use

Read and discuss the following triggers for substance use. Do not limit yourself to the suggested solutions, and add the information you learn about yourself and what might be effective to your skill plans.

- **Feeling a painful emotion:** anxiety, depression, anger, hopelessness, guilt, and shame are just some of the emotions that can lead to substance use.

    - **Solution:** Accept the emotion without judging it, talk to someone supportive, or throw yourself into an activity or distraction. Remember that unhealthy coping of all types feeds painful emotions.

- **Being in a "high-risk" situation:** having yourself surrounded by people, places, and things that you strongly associate with use and/or being in a situation where people are using substances and maybe even pressuring you to do so.

    - **Solution:** Would you stay in a burning building? Figure out how you are going to walk out in a calm and orderly manner, using your skills/plan(s).

- **Having a bad day:** often used as an excuse to escape or take a break from difficulties that come from a tough day.

    - **Solution:** We all need to manage stress on bad days, so develop skills to replace substance use (or other unhealthy ways of coping).

- **Having a great day:** wanting to prolong positive feelings.

    - **Solution:** Brainstorm other ways of keeping the good times going without substances.

- **Reminiscing about the "good old days":** getting nostalgic and not remembering any of the corresponding "bad old days."

    - **Solution:** Gain some balance by recalling the "bad old days," and how substance use has negatively affected you.

- **Minimizing the effects of use:** pushing away how use affects you and others negatively (e.g., thinking that your use is not nearly as bad as others, or that substance use makes you more fun).

    - **Solution:** Think about the long-term effects of use on your life (e.g., with your health, finances, etc.). Remember that you probably have no unique defenses against the long-term effects of substances.

- **Experiencing strong physical sensations and cravings:** some bodily sensations can strongly motivate behavior including substance use.

    - **Solution:** Practice urge-surfing, opposite to emotion, relaxation or distraction. Seek out healthy pleasures and build positive experience.

- **Experiencing withdrawal symptoms:** when you have withdrawal symptoms and feel unwell, it can be tempting to use to feel better again. Beware this vicious cycle!

    - **Solution:** Use radical acceptance with withdrawal symptoms and consult a physician if needed. Immediately practice PLEASED/self-care skills, and try to get into healthy distractions. This discomfort will pass in time.

- **Thinking that one (or one more) won't hurt you:** when in truth you know it definitely will not be just one.

  - **Solution:** Count the times that one was actually one compared to the times it turned out to be more than one, or gather this data going forward.

- **"Reasoning" that this is the last time or that you'll start tomorrow:** although history has proven this to be an unlikely "commitment."

  - **Solution:** Read and talk about stages of change and consider where you are and what you need.

- **Thinking that it's unfair, that other people can do it:** though others don't seem to use with the same frequency, intensity, or duration, or suffer the same ill effects.

  - **Solution:** Radically accept that life is sometimes unfair and mindfully re-focus on skills to build mastery or to build a positive experience without substances.

- **Thinking it's (or you are) a lost cause:** and using substances to "validate" your sense of being worthless.

  - **Solution:** Practice non-judgmental stance, use interpersonal effectiveness to ask for support, or throw yourself into a distraction.

- **Believing you deserve a celebration:** due to an accomplishment.

  - **Solution:** You do deserve a celebration! Think of healthy and positive ways to recognize yourself and your accomplishment.

- **Believing you deserve an escape:** because life has gotten hard.

  - **Solution:** You do deserve an escape! Look at your skills plan or brainstorm with others about healthy pleasures and escapes.

- **Thinking you have to escape this emotion, urge, or situation:** when life seems unbearable.

  - **Solution:** Practice acceptance, distress tolerance skills, or reach out to others for validation and problem-solving. Read this (or another) skills manual until the urge passes (will probably take ten minutes to an hour and you would spend more time seeking, taking, and recovering from a substance).

- **Mixing up your wants and needs:** thinking that wanting substances is the same as needing them.

  - **Solution:** Who "needs" substances other than those who are addicted to them? Get into mindful distractions, relaxation techniques, or other ways to have fun and build positive experience.

- **Myopic thinking:** seeing only a small part of the picture or only today.

  - **Solution:** Get into dialectical thinking, seeing both the forest and the trees.

- **Using a small slip to justify a full-blown relapse:** in for a penny, in for a pound.

  - **Solution:** Actively remember your commitments, use dialectical abstinence, take on a non-judgmental stance, and "play the tape through," considering the likely consequences of a full-blown relapse. Do not burn down a house you worked hard to build.

- **Thinking that no one cares for you anyway:** and you are not worthy of care and concern, so you may as well use.

  - **Solution:** Test that theory by talking to your therapist, another program member, a supportive family member or friend, or with someone at a crisis intervention center or meeting. Be open to allowing someone to show concern, and do not punish their efforts by arguing or rejecting what is offered.

List other triggers to substance use and effective solutions:

Observing and Describing the Effects of Substance Use

Different substances have both different and similar effects on people's lives. The goal of this exercise is to build awareness about the impacts that the substances you use (or have used) have on areas of your life. If you are not sure that the substances you use cause problems for you (or think that they do not), then observe and describe the impacts these substances have on other people who do have problems with them. *Also "fast-forward" and observe and describe concerns you (or others) have about longer-term consequences of your substance use.*

Use information from your therapist(s), program members, books, the internet, discussion, and other sources to complete this exercise. If you are not sure if the information you found is accurate, be sure to inquire further and/or ask someone who knows (e.g., a therapist, physician, or other expert).

Note that this exercise can be done with other problem behaviors too, like chronic suicidal behaviors, self-injury, gambling, over-eating, or any other behaviors that cause undesirable consequences.

Describe how substance use affects the following areas of your life:

Mental Health:

Physical Health:

Spiritual Health:

Family:

Friends:

Education/Self-learning:

Work/Volunteering/Productivity:

Leisure:

Other areas:

Cycle of Emotions and Substance Use

The following page outlines how emotions and substance use follow a cyclical pattern. Notice how vulnerabilities, triggers, emotions and action urges pull us into ineffective behaviors in an attempt to cope. These ineffective behaviors usually fall into two categories: mood-congruent behaviors that maintain mood states or escape and avoidance behaviors to get away from mood states.

These ineffective behaviors often meet short-term needs, but their consequences can intensify the emotions that we needed help with in the first place. Further, these ineffective behaviors can cause other secondary painful emotions like regret, guilt, and shame among others. These consequences then feed into the next vulnerabilities at the top of the cycle. Over time, ineffective coping can become an addiction, where you can become psychologically and/or physically dependent on it.

Study this cycle and use the accompanying handout to identify the specifics of your emotions and substance use cycle. As you complete it, start to think of ways to skillfully intervene at each part of the cycle; each potential problem is an opportunity for practice. Also consider that both substance use and symptoms of mental illness need to be addressed at the same time to effective.

As you learn more about your cycle and its components, consider how you will use that information in your skills plan(s).

Mental Illness and Substance Use Cycle

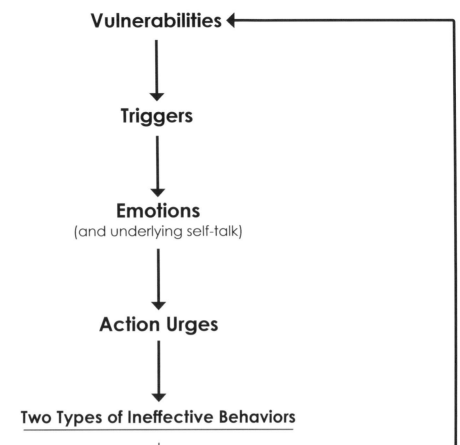

Vulnerabilities

↓

Triggers

↓

Emotions
(and underlying self-talk)

↓

Action Urges

↓

Two Types of Ineffective Behaviors

| **Symptom-oriented Behaviors that Maintain Emotions**
(e.g., isolation, avoidance, decreased self-care, etc.) | **Target Behaviors used to Escape and Avoid Emotions**
(e.g., substance use, self-injury, gambling, etc.) |

Both sets of behaviors can appear to be effective in the *short-term*

↓

Consequences of Ineffective Behaviors
(Includes *long-term* intensification of emotions along with secondary emotional effects)
These Consequences Morph into the Next Set of Vulnerabilities

Observing and Describing a Process of Relapse ——

The following exercise discusses common elements that contribute to a relapse. It is important to know that a relapse is not simply an event but a process. Sometimes this process happens quickly, and at other times it may unfold over days, months, or even longer.

Gaining awareness of how this process unfolds can help you to be proactive in how you can minimize risk and maximize effective coping to stay on track toward your goals. Use your substance use and mental health history and behavior patterns to discover your relapse process and transfer what you discover to your skills plans.

1) Vulnerabilities Thrive

Vulnerabilities frequently begin with a lack of adequate self-care. When people are not getting enough sleep, exercise, and nutrition, it is difficult to be emotionally regulated. If you have cut down or eliminated substance use, the discomfort that comes with withdrawal symptoms is a set-up to relapse without careful attention to helping your body and mind recover (this occasionally happens after a long, sustained period of abstinence too).

Inadequate self-care paired with too much stress (e.g., work, school, financial, housing issues, isolation and/or other relationship problems) can make it especially hard to resist substances.

Additionally, not actively working on creating a satisfying life without substances leaves a lot of opportunities to fall into old behavioral patterns, as does unnecessarily exposing yourself to people, places, situations, and things that are high risk when vulnerabilities are strong.

Describe the vulnerabilities that apply to you, including additional vulnerabilities not listed:

Describe the skills you need to practice to address these vulnerabilities:

2) Strong Feelings, Cravings, and Urges Build

Unchecked vulnerabilities feed strong emotions, especially when people are predisposed to anxiety, depression, anger, or another type of emotion dysregulation. Vulnerabilities also lead to strong cravings and urges, especially if substance use had short-term benefits in the past. In an emotional moment, urges can seem like they last forever.

Describe the feelings, cravings, and urges that can be difficult to manage:

Describe the skills you need to practice to address these feelings, cravings, and urges:

3) Thinking about Substance Use Becomes a Preoccupation

At this part of the process people can become preoccupied with substance use. You may minimize or rationalize using or get into another type of "stuck thinking" that will not work for you. You may convince yourself that substance use will work and not be any big deal, "just this time." Or you may tell yourself that it is hopeless and does not matter anyway.

Describe what you have told yourself in your mind (i.e., your self-talk) about substance use before a relapse happens. Also describe how your self-talk at those times appears to you in retrospect:

Describe the skills you need to practice to address this self-talk:

4) Planning a Relapse in Your Mind

At some point thinking might shift into planning. What are you going to use, where will it happen, who will you be with, or how will you plan the time you need to do it alone? How will you keep it secret or minimize it to others? At this point you are practicing in your mind what does not work in your life.

Describe how your planning at those times appears to you in retrospect:

Describe the skills you need to practice to address "mental planning":

5) Putting Your Plans into Motion

At this point you are taking active steps to use substances. You decide to drive to the liquor store or to call a friend who is "holding." You call in sick to work and go to a bar, or you take some other behavioral steps. While each of these steps is an opportunity to change course and make a u-turn, the farther you go down this road, the more difficult it is to avoid a SLIP.

At this stage you are in emotion and addiction mind, and need to work toward Wise and Clear Mind.

Describe how putting your plans into motion at those times appears to you in retrospect:

Describe the skills you need to practice to address behavioral steps toward use:

6) Having a SLIP

A SLIP is the final destination in this process: This is actual use. The task now is to revisit dialectical abstinence as soon as possible, to quickly repair the mistake, and to learn from it as you recommit to your goals. A step in a different, skillful direction in needed.

Describe what you have learned from your SLIPs and how it can improve your progress:

Describe the skills you need to practice to minimize and/or avoid SLIPs:

Breathing: The Anchor to Mindfulness

Breathing is the essence of life and the most fundamental anchor to come mindfully back to the present moment. Breathing can also be considered to be an "incompatible skill" in that practicing it is directly incompatible with many problem emotions, urges, and behaviors. Once you have practiced breathing, you will find that it counters stress, anxiety, anger, and impulsivity--all issues that commonly contribute to substance use.

There is an Eastern belief that each person has a finite number of breaths, and once that amount is used, the person dies. While this belief is not literally true, it does reflect a great deal of wisdom. If you breathe quickly and shallowly, you never get the optimum amount of oxygen into your body, and your systems run inefficiently, causing a greater load and stress on your body (and you use your finite breaths quickly!). Alternatively, if you practice breathing slowly and deeply, you get the oxygen you need, your systems run better, and not only do you decrease stress, but you find peace and serenity.

Practicing more effective breathing is free, takes relatively little time, and can be done anywhere. To reap its rewards, you must practice breathing exercises at least a few times a day, and dedicate some effort to developing this skill. Remember to be non-judgmental when you practice breathing; the whole point is to engage acceptance by breathing into the moment.

Breathing Exercises

Practice at least one of these exercises at least three times a day and when you feel a strong emotion, have a judgmental thought, or when you feel impulsive or experience an urge. Observe and describe your level of distress before and after each exercise.

- **3-5-7 Breathing Technique:** Start by exhaling completely. Then inhale through your nose for a count of three, hold it for a count of five, and completely exhale through the mouth for a count of seven. Do not be afraid of making a little noise as you exhale!

- **Counting Breaths:** Breathe in and say "one" as you exhale, then continue breathing and counting on each exhalation until you reach 10. Once you reach 10 (or if you lose your count), go back to one. Do this exercise for three to five minutes.

- **Cue to Breathe:** Decide on five to 10 stimuli in your environment that will now "cue" you to take one to three deep breaths. Possible examples of cues to breath include:

    □ seeing a certain color

    □ having your child misbehave

    □ seeing someone you don't like (or do like)

    □ walking through a doorway

    □ being at a red light

    □ sitting at your computer or workstation

- **Frustration to Peace:** As a variation of the above exercise, pick five common frustrating events that will cue you to breathe deeply. Remember also to practice being non-judgmental and to accept the moment. Try repeating a mantra such as "life is like this" along with your breathing.

- **Bellows Technique:** Breathe rapidly in and out through your nose, trying to get three cycles of inhaling and exhaling in per second. Continue for 10 seconds. This technique is designed to stimulate and give an energy boost.

- **Alternate Nostril:** Hold your left nostril closed and breathe in through your right nostril; then open your left nostril and hold your right nostril closed while you breathe out through the left nostril. Breathe back in through your left nostril, and continue the exercise alternating back and forth. This technique is designed to bring balance.

- **Square Breathing** (Moonshine, 2008): Breathe in for four seconds, hold it for four seconds, breath out for four seconds, repeat four times.

Distress Tolerance Module

Distress tolerance skills replace unhealthy behaviors used to escape, avoid, or otherwise attempt to cope with painful emotions, situations, and crises.

We all have times in life in which we feel overwhelmed and need relief. Sometimes people have learned to cope through using substances, or through other behaviors like over-eating, self-injury, gambling, and/or spending too much money, among other behaviors. While these types of behaviors "solve" the problem in the short-term, they often cause more distress and problems in the long-term, being self-defeating.

It is difficult to give up any behavior without replacing it with something new. The goal of distress tolerance skills is to build a new repertoire of behaviors to replace ways of coping that have lost their usefulness or that have lead to other kinds of distress and problems.

As you learn and practice the skills in this module, add them to your *Substance Use Prevention Plan,* your *Mental Health Symptom Response Plan,* and your *Health Maintenance Plan.* The goal of distress tolerance is to have a full toolbox to handle any type of emotion, problem, or crisis that occurs in your life.

Distress Tolerance Guidelines for Use

The effectiveness of distress tolerance is based on knowing when to use these skills and recognizing their limitations. The guidelines listed here identify situations in which distress tolerance is indicated and also to maximize its effectiveness:

1. **Use distress tolerance when you cannot solve a problem and feel like using substances, acting on urges to harm yourself, or doing anything else that is self-sabotaging.** If you are able to solve your problem, it is an okay time to do so, and you are sufficiently in Wise Mind to do so, then take care of the problem. Otherwise, use distress tolerance.

2. **Develop your distress tolerance skills and plan before you need them.** Similar to protocols and drills people practice in other emergency situations like fires, dangerous weather, and other crises, you need to know your protocols and drills to follow when crisis happens to you. Plan to be proactive in tolerating distress, and practice your plans! Practicing distress tolerance can keep you in Wise and Clear Mind.

3. **Continue to diversify your distress tolerance skills.** You cannot have too many options available. Do not get complacent in developing these skills...work to master as many as possible. The more tools you have, the better, especially since many of these skills are short-term strategies.

4. **When a particular skill does not work, step back and see what is missing.** Maybe you need to use mindfulness too, maybe you have "burnt out" the effectiveness of that skill, or maybe you just need to switch strategies. If so, change it up. If you cannot get over the mountain, walk around it. Sometimes it is not about trying harder, but trying differently.

5. **Do not give up.** Coach yourself, ask for help, and be responsive (not reactive) to the realities of the situation.

ACCEPTS

Wise Mind allows us to accept distress and orients us toward these skills

Use the acronym **ACCEPTS** to remember the building blocks of this skill: (Activities, Contributing, Comparisons, Emotions, Push Away, Thoughts, Sensations). These building blocks are described in further detail in the paragraphs that follow.

Activities: Activities give you alternatives to substance use, decrease depression, anxiety, and other mental health symptoms, and can create positive emotions. The more invigorating the activity, the better. Throw yourself mindfully into activities without expecting or clinging to certain outcomes. The outcomes take care of themselves when you are on the journey.

Think of all the time dedicated to seeking substances, using them, and recovering from them and/or the time spent stuck in mental health symptoms. You need other stuff to do!

Plan and schedule activities as part of your daily routine and follow through with the plans. Consult the Activities List that follows ACCEPTS.

Contributing: Contributing helps you get out of yourself and your distress and into participating with others and in the world. We all need a break from ourselves, and contributing creates connection and positive feelings.

Assist other people in overcoming their symptoms and in their recovery by being available, supportive, and sharing ideas. Contribute by walking the walk, and being a model for other people.

Comparisons: Comparisons keep us from falling into a dark place through bringing balance and perspective. You can compare yourself to other times when you struggled more or been less effective with skills. You can also compare yourself to others with greater problems than you. Even though you may have it tough, other people have been dealt an even worse hand.

Emotions: Seek out activities, events, and thoughts that create different feelings. Remember that emotions can be influenced by what you choose to do and what you choose to think about.

Listen to music that creates different emotions: loud and fast music when fatigued, calming music when anxious or upset, or uplifting music when sad. Watch favorite shows or movies, fondly remember fun times (without comparing them to your current situation), or work on a project.

Push Away: Push away distress by mentally locking it in a box and putting it on a shelf in a locked room. Make the imagery as vivid as possible, practicing it over and over. Say: "This is a tomorrow problem" and then focus on something else. Or, write down something about the problem and put it away in a drawer or someplace where you will find it when you are ready.

Remember to take out your problem at a safe time to attend to it. Pushing-away is a short-term strategy.

Thoughts: Mindfully focus on distracting thoughts. You can only think about one thing at a time, and your distress will diminish when you focus on other thoughts. The classic example is counting to 10 when angry; thinking about something else (counting) helps us to cool down and be more rational.

Read a magazine or book, do Sudoku or other puzzles, think about inspirational sayings and quotes, listen to the lyrics in music, get into a great conversation, or watch a movie.

Sensations: Sensations include anything that is physically vigorous or actively awakens your senses. The skill is different from the Self-Soothe skills in that it seeks to stimulate rather than relax.

Take a brisk walk or engage in exercise, such as running, swimming, or weight-lifting. Get into a hot or cold bath or shower or splash cold water on your face. Engage your senses with loud music, bold colors, or strong tastes or smells.

Getting Busy with Activities

Symptoms of mental illness and substance use take up a lot of time. As you start to address these issues, you may find that you need to fill that time with healthy and beneficial activities. Below is a list of pleasant activities, many of which are free. Add specific pleasant activities to the list that you enjoy. Make sure to schedule at least three pleasant activities each day. Also, remember to use mindfulness skills with each experience.

1. Go for a walk, jog, or run
2. Fix or ride a bike
3. Watch lectures on YouTube®
4. Refinish furniture
5. Sit on a park bench and people-watch
6. Browse magazines or books at the library
7. Play board games
8. Have a snack mindfully
9. Appreciate a favorite actor or act yourself
10. Read the Bible or other religious text
11. Advocate for the National Alliance on Mental Illness (NAMI), a political cause, or the environment
12. Stargaze, find constellations, or wonder about the universe

Read about animals or visit the zoo
13. Appreciate the arts or create your own
14. Play badminton
15. Redecorate or rearrange your house
16. Join a group
17. Have a conversation with a friend or a stranger
18. Watch or play baseball or softball
19. Make crafts
20. Watch, read about, or fly an airplane or build a model
21. Watch or play basketball or play HORSE
22. Bathe or shower mindfully
23. Relax at (or imagine being at) the beach; look for shells or clean up the beach
24. Do beadwork
25. Beatbox, rap, or sing
26. Ring a bell
27. Breathe mindfully

28. Write a short story
29. Bike
30. Feed or watch birds
31. Blog or visit blogs
32. Boat
33. Bowl
34. Bet a *small* amount of money (if you have no gambling issues)
35. Start a fantasy football league (or join one)
36. Play checkers
37. Help the disabled
38. Contribute at a food pantry
39. Bake a cake and decorate it
40. Go geocaching
41. Do calligraphy
42. Camp
43. Make candles or ice candles
44. Canoe
45. Have a picnic in your home
46. Read about cars or go for a drive
47. Do some cheerleading
48. Take a nap
49. Watch one television show mindfully
50. Window-shop (without spending)
51. Play chess
52. Go to church and associated activities
53. Watch clouds
54. Make a sand castle
55. Collect coins
56. Go to an antique shop to browse
57. Collect artwork

58. Collect albums or CDs or look at and listen to old ones
59. Compose music or lyrics
60. Look at architecture in magazines or around town
61. Enjoy perfume or cologne
62. Do computer activities
63. Cook
64. Crochet
65. Cross-stitch
66. Do a crossword puzzle
67. Dance anywhere
68. Play darts (not lawn darts)
69. Look at your collectibles
70. Bowl with friends or in a league
71. Daydream
72. Juggle
73. Play dominoes or set them up to let them fall
74. Draw
75. Eat out or fix a special meal at home
76. Take a community education course or educate yourself on a new topic
77. Tinker with electronics
78. Do embroidery
79. Entertain others
80. Exercise: aerobics, weights, yoga
81. Go fishing
82. Watch or play football
83. Take a hot or cool shower
84. Tell jokes and laugh
85. Go four-wheeling
86. Paint a wall
87. Enjoy or maintain an aquarium
88. Play Frisbee® or disc golf
89. Mend clothes
90. Have a spirited debate (without needing to be right)
91. Join a club

92. Play games
93. Garden
94. Swim
95. Keep a dream journal
96. Hug a friend or family member
97. Visit garage sales
98. Be intimate with a loved one
99. Be a mentor
100. Build a bird house
101. Do genealogy
102. Walk your (or a neighbor's) dog
103. Visit an art museum
104. Go to the movies or watch a favorite DVD
105. Golf
106. Practice putting
107. Give yourself a facial
108. Paint a picture or finger-paint
109. Watch funny YouTube® videos (or post one)
110. Find an activity listed more than once on this list
111. Go go-kart racing
112. Play Texas Hold 'Em
113. Volunteer at the Humane Society
114. Write a letter to the editor
115. Light a candle and enjoy the smell or the flame
116. Play video games
117. Scrapbook
118. Become a pen pal
119. Support any cause
120. Play guitar
121. Write a handwritten letter
122. Hike
123. Do home repair
124. Breathe in fresh air
125. Build a home theater system
126. Record your favorite shows and watch back-to-back
127. Air drum or air guitar to a cool song

128. Ride a horse
129. Write a thank-you letter
130. Hunt
131. Surf the Internet
132. Fix a bike
133. Make jewelry
134. Browse your favorite store
135. Put together a jigsaw puzzle
136. Build a fort with your kids
137. Journal
138. Juggle
139. Kayak
140. See life like a young child
141. Say a prayer
142. Build or fly kites
143. Knit
144. Tie knots
145. Sing a silly song
146. Pick flowers
147. Learn anything new
148. Learn a foreign language
149. Practice telling a joke
150. Learn an instrument
151. Listen to music
152. Macramé
153. Color with kids (or without)
154. Smile at someone
155. Be affectionate
156. Do a magic trick
157. Meditate
158. Use a metal detector
159. Teach a child something
160. Build models
161. Ride or look at motorcycles
162. Play with children
163. Go mountain biking

164. Work with a team
165. Plant an herb garden
166. Go to a community center
167. Grow a Chia® pet
168. Climb a mountain
169. Make a root beer float
170. Lie in the grass
171. Scrapbook
172. Practice a musical instrument
173. Needlepoint
174. Read reviews on a topic of interest
175. Do Origami
176. Play Trivial Pursuit® or any trivia game
177. Clean out a closet and donate unneeded items
178. Plan a movie marathon
179. Look at StumbleUpon.com
180. Join a chat room
181. Play paintball
182. Go to a water park
183. Share something thoughtful found on the Internet
184. Go to a video arcade
185. Indulge in a guilty pleasure
186. Email friends and family
187. Join a drum circle
188. Rollerblade
189. Swing at a playground
190. Go to the mall to walk or browse (without spending)
191. Water your plants
192. Make a collage
193. Hang with a friend
194. Listen to music and read the lyrics
195. Try a new recipe
196. Paint your nails
197. Sit by any body of water
198. Go to the library

199.Organize a neighborhood garden

200.Groom a pet

201.Watch a sunrise or sunset

202.Take a walk

203.Go the a health club or YMCA

204.Go to a coffee shop

List the activities you like (or have liked) to do:

Circle at least 10 new activities from the list that you are willing to try.

Describe how these activities will help you manage mental illness and substance use issues:

Activities Worksheet

Activities provide healthy distractions and create enjoyment. Getting active alleviates the symptoms of mental illness and provides alternatives to substance use. Use this worksheet to list activities you plan to do today. Notice how you feel before and after each activity.

☐ _____

Distress/urge level before:_____ Distress/urge level after:_____

☐ _____

Distress/urge level before:_____ Distress/urge level after:_____

☐ _____

Distress/urge level before:_____ Distress/urge level after:_____

☐ _____

Distress/urge level before:_____ Distress/urge level after:_____

☐ _____

Distress/urge level before:_____ Distress/urge level after:_____

☐ _____

Distress/urge level before:_____ Distress/urge level after:_____

☐ _____

Distress/urge level before:_____ Distress/urge level after:_____

IMPROVE the Moment

Like ACCEPTS, these skills provide healthy distractions.

Use the acronym **IMPROVE** to remember the building blocks (Imagery, Meaning, Prayer, Relaxation, One thing or step at a time, Vacation, Encouragement) of this skill. These building blocks are described in further detail in the paragraphs that follow.

Imagery: Harness the power of positive imagery to feel better and more relaxed. Concentrate on a scene in your mind (a beach, the forest, a safe and happy place) and concentrate on it or practice guided imagery with a CD. Your mind will convince your body that it is there, slowing your breathing, dropping your blood pressure, relaxing your muscles, and slightly increasing your body temperature.

Rehearse skill use in your mind's eye, seeing yourself cope or perform effectively. Imagine what your life will be like when you are sober, feeling good, and accomplishing your goals. Envision specifically what your satisfying life will be like.

Consider practicing imagery before bedtime as part of your sleep routine. Remember to never practice in your mind what does not work in your life (e.g., misuse imagery by imagining substance use or other harmful behavior).

Meaning: Contemplate what you might gain from this struggle. Sometimes tremendous growth and wisdom springs from adversity. Is this a tragedy or "great practice"? Is it a problem or an opportunity? Many people who have struggled with addictions consider themselves grateful for the experience and the lessons learned. Perhaps struggling with addiction and mental illness has shown you that you can be resourceful and overcome great obstacles. Dialectically, every downside has an upside.

Prayer: Pray for strength and resolve in distressful times. Seek connection with and guidance from your higher power. Avoid "why me" or bargaining prayers; those prayers tend to demoralize us rather than build us up.

As an alternative, "talk" to anyone important to you: A deceased relative you loved, a person you admire (whether you know him/her or not), or anyone who helps you feel connected outside yourself.

If you have found Twelve-Step programs helpful, you might understand the power of this skill.

Relaxation: Practice breathing exercises (see Mindfulness), Self-Soothe skills, progressive muscle relaxation with each major muscle group, or anything that calms you.

Because many people use substances to relax, it is paramount to find other ways of meeting this human need and to build it into your daily routine.

One Thing or Step at a Time: When overwhelmed, go back to the most important priority again and again. If you have many problems, pick the most important one to focus on or the one you have the most resources to solve. Sometimes we need to accept having many problems to solve one.

One thing or step at a time is vital in recovery. You may not know how to stay clean for a week, but you probably can for a day, or an hour, or a minute. Commit to the time period that you can successfully manage and continue to renew your commitment in increments. Take one thing at a time, one step at a time.

Vacation: Vacation means taking a break when we are in distress (or before we are in distress). Step outside, breathe fresh air, and take a short walk. Spend ten minutes listening to music or surfing the Internet. Exercise, engage in a hobby, talk with a friend, or watch your favorite shows. Plan "you" time everyday in one way or another.

If substance use has been your way of taking a vacation or break, you have to find new ways of meeting this need, and you need to address the need proactively, not just as a distress tolerance skill.

Remember that this is intended to be a time-limited break and not long-term avoidance.

Encouragement: Notice the content of your self-talk, non-judgmentally. Gently let go of discouraging statements and replace them with coping and encouraging statements such as:

"I can do this."

"I have friends who care about me."

"I can survive this next minute."

"I'm doing the best I can."

"Skills can help me now."

"This is happening to teach me patience (or some other virtue)"

The content of our thoughts has tremendous influence, so do not just let those old tapes play. Create some new music.

Burning Bridges: Remove the Means of Acting on Urges to Use and Other Harmful Behaviors

Bridge-burning refers to actively removing the means of acting on your urges to use substances or act on other harmful behaviors. The concept of bridge-burning recognizes that relapse into harmful behaviors happens more easily when there is the immediate opportunity to act on impulses. Eliminating the opportunities and/or inserting barriers between urge and action will result in more opportunities to practice skills.

Bridge-Burning with Substance Use:

- Remove all alcohol and drugs from your home

- Remove all alcohol- and drug-related objects and paraphernalia from your home (e.g., cocktail glasses, corkscrew, pipes, papers, lighters, and/or anything associated with use)

- Erase the numbers of using friends, associates, and dealers from your phone

- Block the phone numbers of using friends, associates, and dealers from your phone or get a new number

- Stay away from bars, liquor stores, and locations associated with use, changing your routines and routes to actively avoid them

- Do not carry cash

- Tell anyone and everyone that you have given up substances

- Actively tell others when you experience urges to use

List other ways to burn bridges to substance use:

Bridge-Burning with Self-Injury and/or Suicidal Urges:

- Remove razors, lighters, and other self-injury tools

- Mix up and change rituals associated with self-injury

- Remove the specific method of acting on suicide

- Tell others when you are unsafe and need help

- Go to the hospital <u>before</u> acting on suicidal urges

List other ways of bridge-burning with self-injury and/or suicidal urges:

Bridge-Burning with Spending:

- Cut up credit cards (if you need to keep one, freeze it in water so it will take longer to access it or have someone trustworthy hold it for you)

- Have someone trustworthy keep extra money when urges are high

- Establish a "waiting period" before making a decision to buy any non-essential item

- Stay away from stores, the mall, online shopping, and/or TV shopping

List other ways of bridge-burning with spending:

Bridge-Burning with Unhealthy and/or Hopeless Relationships:

- Erase the other person's number from your phone

- Block the other person's number or get a new number

- Route emails from the other person to your "junk mail folder"

- Tell anyone and everyone that you have moved on from the relationship

- Fill your free time with activities and healthy people

List other ways of bridge-burning with hopeless relationships:

Bridge-Burning with Overeating:

- Keep binge and "comfort" foods out of your home

- Dish out your portions and put the rest away before eating

- Eat multiple times a day, mindfully, including healthy snacks

List other ways of bridge-burning with overeating:

Bridge-Burning with Gambling:

- Avoid places were gambling occurs

- Limit your access to cash and credit that can be used for gambling.

- Have someone trustworthy hold onto your money when urges are high

- Block internet access to gambling websites

List other ways of bridge-burning with gambling:

Bridge-burning works best in conjunction with other skills. When we remove the ability to act on harmful behaviors, we need to replace them with something new and skillful. ***Be careful not to trade one unhealthy behavior for another.***

Urge Surfing: Ride the Wave

Urge surfing is the non-judgmental acceptance of urges that allows you to simply notice and ride their ebbs and flows without reaction.

The essence of urge surfing is to understand that urges are a part of our experience and are not commands for action. Often, instead of just watching our urges, we unwittingly intensify them. Judging and catastrophizing are two ways in which we make it harder on ourselves to tolerate urges. We have a natural tendency to want to escape urges we judge to be intolerable by fighting them or acting on them. Both of these approaches to urges ultimately intensify them.

Trying to fight urges is not unlike struggling to escape quicksand: Frantic efforts lead to sinking. Like fighting urges, escaping discomfort by acting on urges will also cause you to go under in time. This happens because relieving tension with unhealthy behaviors is reinforcing and feeds the cycle of urges followed by ineffective actions.

The secret is to not panic and react, but to float. Riding the ebbs and flows requires us to be willing to have a non-judgmental relationship with our urges, even when they cause intense discomfort. It may seem counter-intuitive, but an acceptance-based relationship with urges, emotions, or any other uncomfortable experience will decrease the intensity of many of these experiences over time. Remember that acceptance is not resignation; instead it is a state of mind in which we acknowledge "what is," freeing up our resources to be responsive and effective.

Practice urge surfing when your urges are at lower levels. Like real surfing, you learn to ride smaller waves before you can graduate to large swells, and you also learn when the waves are too intense to ride. Keep in mind that urge surfing works well in combination with other skills, such as distraction. Be responsive and switch up skill strategies based on what works.

Self-Soothe: Calming Your Mind and Body ———

Tension and anxiety often intensify substance use urges and symptoms of mental illness. Relaxation is a key to recovery and self-soothing is one way to practice relaxation. Self-soothe is the mindful connection to pleasant experiences through our senses. Practicing self-soothe daily will increase peace and serenity in your life, and you will notice the corresponding effects in your body including decreased heart rate, blood pressure, slower and deeper breathing, and muscle relaxation.

Self-soothe with the senses includes the following examples:

Sight: Look at your surroundings and notice the details. Attend and linger on what is visually pleasing. It may be art, architecture, nature, or simply seeing the beauty in our everyday surroundings.

List how you can use self-soothe with sight:

Hearing: Listen to sounds that are relaxing, perhaps closing your eyes to focus in on them. Notice the sounds all around you that have their own beauty and rhythm. Put on music or listen to the sound of running water or a crackling fire.

List how you can use self-soothe with hearing:

Smell: Breathe in deeply scents that calm and soothe. Notice the pleasant scents of people, places, and things that you enjoy. Breathe in the aromas of the food you eat.

List how you can use self-soothe with smell:

Taste: Eat and drink everything you consume mindfully, paying full attention to the complex tastes and textures of what you eat and drink. Remember not to eat and drink mindlessly and excessively. The goal is to get maximum enjoyment from small amounts of food and drink. Also, strive to use self-soothe with taste with healthy and nutritious fare.

List how you can self-soothe with taste:

Touch: Feel that which creates pleasant bodily sensations: comfortable clothing, a plush chair, a warm or cool breeze, the warmth of the sun, the softness of a pet, or the touch of someone you love.

List how you can self-soothe with touch:

Multisensory: Mindfully activate and attend to each sense when you eat at a restaurant (or create a restaurant experience in your home), go to a movie, visit a park, or have any other potentially engaging experience.

List how you can self-soothe by combining your senses:

Mind Sense: Engage in peaceful thoughts, affirmations, and meditations as well as daydreams and fantasies. Focus your mind, complete with imagery, on that which creates serenity.

List how you can self-soothe by engaging in your mental processes:

Spiritual Sense: Connect with your higher power, your spirituality, or with nature. Tapping into a spiritual sense can create peace, serenity, and well-being, especially through mindful reflections, rituals, and contemplation.

List how you can self-soothe by engaging in your sense of spirituality:

Many people do not practice self-soothe because of barriers. Recognize if you have any of these common barriers and note the challenges to these barriers that follow them.

- **Barrier:** Thinking that you do not have time to self-soothe.

  Challenge: Think about how much time seeking, taking, and recovering from substance use and/or being stuck in symptoms of mental illness takes. Spending 20 minutes a day to self-soothe is an excellent trade!

- **Barrier:** Thinking that you have more important responsibilities to do.

  Challenge: Think about how more efficient and effective you will be when you approach life in a more relaxed manner.

- **Barrier:** Thinking that you do not deserve to self-soothe and/or have not earned it.

  Challenges: 1. Having a more relaxed life will help you to better reach your goals. 2. Having a more relaxed life is more of a human right than something that must be deserved or earned.

- **Barrier:** Feeling guilty when you self-soothe (often in connection with one of the thought barriers above).

  Challenge: Coach yourself with self-talk by saying its "ok" and even desirable to self-soothe and then practice it over and over until you can self-soothe without guilt (this is opposite to emotion).

- **Barrier:** Struggling with mindfulness and being frustrated or overwhelmed by distractions.

  Challenge: Remind yourself that distractions are part of the world and that struggles with mindfulness are opportunities to practice.

Distress Tolerance Worksheet ─────────────

Many people develop a few distress tolerance skills and then quit actively exploring and practicing new skills. Just as carpenters, computer programmers, artists, mechanics, students, therapists, and other people work to acquire new tools and techniques, you need to continue to work on new Distress Tolerance skills to be effective in challenging situations. Use the checklist spaces below to list new Distress Tolerance skills to practice today or this week, and be sure to check them off after you have practiced them. Notice how you feel before and after each Distress Tolerance skill.

☐ _____

Distress/urge level before:_____ Distress/urge level after:_____

☐ _____

Distress/urge level before:_____ Distress/urge level after:_____

☐ _____

Distress/urge level before:_____ Distress/urge level after:_____

☐ _____

Distress/urge level before:_____ Distress/urge level after:_____

☐ _____

Distress/urge level before:_____ Distress/urge level after:_____

☐ _____

Distress/urge level before:_____ Distress/urge level after:_____

☐ _____

Distress/urge level before:_____ Distress/urge level after:_____

Pros and Cons (P&C)

Pros and Cons is a reason mind exercise to counter-balance strong emotions and urges. After completing a thorough Pros and Cons, many people find themselves solidly in Wise Mind and ready to act responsively.

Further, if we use Pros and Cons to decide whether we want to engage in substance use or another harmful behavior, we will frequently find that urges subside by the time the exercise is complete. To use this skill, start by identifying your basic choices. Examples include drinking or using drugs versus staying sober, using self-injury versus staying safe, and practicing an old behavior versus practicing a skill.

When you have identified the basic choices, plug them into the worksheet that follows. After you have determined both short- and long-term pros and cons, check to see if you are in Wise Mind and make a decision. If you find that you are not in Wise Mind, table your decision and try another skill.

Pros and Cons Worksheet

Short-Term PROS of _____   Short-Term CONS of _____

Long-Term PROS of _____   Long-Term CONS of _____

VERSUS

Short-Term PROS of _____   Short-Term CONS of _____

Long-Term PROS of _____   Long-Term CONS of _____

Grounding Yourself

Grounding exercises bring us back to the present moment when we struggle with dissociation or with feeling unreal. Dissociation is a natural way of coping when faced with extreme danger or being hurt. However, leaving reality is less effective when we are distressed but not in imminent harm and, after a while, this manner of coping actively interferes with life.

Practice these exercises proactively and mindfully, and they will decrease symptoms of dissociation and derealization. These grounding techniques can also be used to cope with painful emotions and intense urges.

- Open your eyes and observe and describe your surroundings in detail.

- Who or what is around you? You are here, now. The more detail, no matter how minor, the better.

- Work your senses: Name what you see, hear, smell, and touch right here and now, again using as many details as possible.

- Use the Sensations skill from ACCEPTS. Practice the different variations of Sensations.

- Observe your body in contact with your chair. Feel your back, behind, and back of your legs in connection with the chair. Feel your arms in connection with the armrests or your lap. Feel your feet firmly planted on the ground. Now think about how your body is connected to the chair, which is connected to the floor, which is connected to the building, which is connected to the earth.

- Breathe slowly and deeply, counting your breaths.

- Get up and stretch out, feeling your body and moving about.

- Repeat a mantra like "this is now and not then."

List other ways to ground yourself:

Radical Acceptance

Many people have great pain due to trauma, difficult life circumstances, and losses. Pain is an inevitable part of life, but it can seem impossible to accept. Pain is also created when people do not want to accept problems with substances, frequently because substance use is meeting important needs. Unfortunately, meeting those needs through substances becomes self-defeating and harmful once the immediate needs have been gratified.

If we are unable to accept situations that cause pain and are self-defeating, the result is being stuck and trapped in chronic suffering that can no longer be covered up. The refusal to accept and connect with our suffering creates unending suffering. Counter-intuitively, we decrease suffering by being willing to accept it and relate to it rather than fight it. We may have to tolerate pain, but there will be a qualitative difference in our experience of it.

An old recovery adage (that also applies to mental health symptoms) is "when nothing changes, nothing changes." Acceptance instead of resistance releases our resources to move forward, so something can finally change.

It is helpful to know that Radical Acceptance is a process similar to Kubler-Ross's (2005) stages of acceptance:

1. **Denial:** not believing our loss, problem, or situation is real.

2. **Anger:** being angry about why this has or is happening to us.

3. **Bargaining**: trying to make a deal with someone or a higher power to change reality, or telling yourself you will only use on certain days, or at certain times, or that this use will be your last time.

4. **Depression:** feeling despondent as reality sets in.

5. **Acceptance:** acknowledging reality without fighting it.

These stages do not always unfold step-wise and sequentially. Instead, we commonly go back and forth, sometimes getting stuck in one stage and/or skipping others. When you experience these stages and emotions, you are in the process of acceptance and, by definition, in the process of change. Similar to the stages of change, each stage of acceptance has its own purpose and lessons, and just like changing a problem behavior, acceptance can lead to freedom.

Everyday Acceptance

Radical Acceptance is the skill used to deal with painful and difficult-to-accept situations. Everyday Acceptance orients us to the practice of acceptance as a lifestyle. The daily practice of acceptance is necessary to maintaining mental health and abstinence, knowing that painful feelings and urges to use substances feed on willfulness, resistance, and fighting reality. What does everyday acceptance mean? Consider these examples:

- Experiencing an uncomfortable feeling or urge without reaction

- Recognizing that life is sometimes spelled "HASSLE" (in the words of Albert Ellis)

- Being last in line

- Knowing that getting drunk or high is not an option for you anymore (this would likely be radical acceptance early in recovery!)

- Having someone share a criticism with you

- Being out of shape

- Having crabby, unappreciative, or disrespectful people around you

- Being behind on the laundry, dishes, or some other important task

- Losing your keys

- Wanting to get high and knowing you cannot (for all the reasons)

- Having to work when you do not want to

- Missing out on something fun

- Feeling an increase in symptoms

- Having your car, bike, or other mode of transportation break down

Do not confuse this approach to everyday life as being resigned, being walked on, or remaining helpless. Many of these problems require active solutions and skill use (although some may simply be acceptance issues). The use of everyday acceptance allows us to have the emotional balance to solve problems more effectively through reducing the emotional energy and load we often lump on them. Acceptance is not resignation, but empowerment!

Willingness (W) Versus Willfulness

Willingness means doing what is necessary to meet the demands of the situation we are in, assessing what is needed and responding without getting caught in judgments. It means adopting an attitude of acceptance and side-stepping emotions that create willfulness (e.g., self-righteousness, pride, fear, doubt) in order to meet reality with effective action.

Life does not unfold according to our preferences and expectations; in many situations we do not choose the cards we are dealt. Willingness involves playing the hand you have to your best ability, using all of your resources and removing your own barriers to reach whatever outcome is desired.

We frequently know what is needed but resist it anyways, for a lot of different reasons. Resistance to reality, and the refusal to play the hand you are dealt is willfulness. Willfulness can be bold, like acting in a way that blatantly sabotages your own self-interest to "show" others, and willfulness can be subtle, like making quiet, seemingly unnoticed choices that slowly erode your goals and what you want in life.

Identifying a willful state of mind is the first step toward willingness. Once you acknowledge willfulness as being a barrier with any situation, you can begin to identify what would be effective to reach your goals. Contrary to the Western idea, "Where there is a will, there is a way," you want to adopt the philosophy: "Where there is willingness, there is a way."

This philosophy speaks to the common misconception that using your "will" or "will power" to cope, stay sober, control a situation, or reach some other desired outcome will be helpful. Do not confuse the idea of "willing oneself" with "being willing," and strive for the latter.

Willingness, like acceptance, brings greater peace, serenity, control, and effectiveness to life.

Emotion Regulation Module

Emotion regulation skills reduce our vulnerability to extreme feelings and urges to use substances. A common acronym in the treatment of substance use is HALT, which stands for Hungry, Angry, Lonely, and Tired. It is well known that these states make one vulnerable to using (and other problems), and there are skills in this module to address each of them.

An initial goal of emotion regulation is to identify and understand how feelings occur and how they can be influenced by changing events and how we interpret them. Knowledge about our emotions can be empowering.

Along with understanding our emotions, we want to change our relationship to them. Instead of judging or attempting to "get rid" of negative emotions, the practice of accepting, listening to, and having a relationship with emotions leads to soothing them and reducing emotional suffering.

Effective self-care is a cornerstone of emotion regulation. It is nearly impossible to feel emotionally healthy if basic physical self-care is not practiced daily. Balanced eating and sleeping (as evidenced in the HALT acronym) is essential to feeling good, as is exercise and taking care of physical illness when it comes up.

Lastly, emotion regulation is based on having enough positive events scheduled in life as well as learning how to step out of mood-congruent behaviors that are self-defeating, like isolating when depressed and avoiding when anxious.

Understanding Emotions

An understanding of emotions gives us the knowledge necessary to influence them. The diagram below outlines how emotions happen. Note that events and how we interpret events has a significant impact on what we feel.

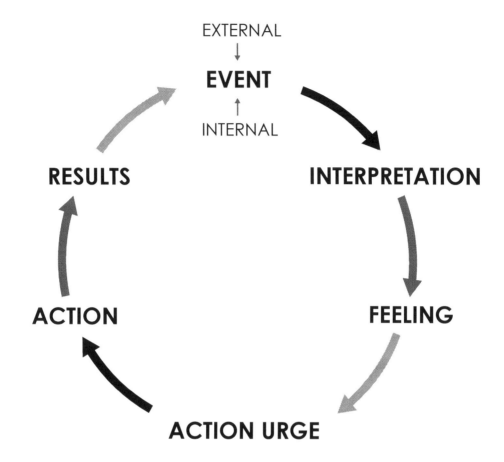

Event: Emotions start with events that can be internal (within us) or external (in our environment).

Interpretation: Our interpretation of an event is pivotal in the resulting emotion. Refer to some of the ways we get stuck with thinking in the next handout to work with your self-talk.

Emotion: Use your mindfulness skills to connect with your emotional experience. What is happening in your body (e.g., muscle relaxation or tension, heart rate, breathing)? What is happening externally with what your body is communicating (e.g., facial expressions, posture)? Based on this information, try to give a name to your emotion.

Action Urge: What is your emotion pulling you to do (or not do)? Remember that we are not our emotions or urges, and they do not always require action!

Action: What are you doing (or not doing)?

Results: What are the effective and ineffective consequences of your actions? How do these consequences benefit you or create vulnerabilities that will influence the next event?

Effective Thinking: Shifting and Expanding Interpretations of Events

Our emotions affect our thinking, and our thinking affects our emotions. An interpretation is an internal behavior that determines the meaning of an event, and that meaning depends on perspective. To be most effective, it is important not to be stuck in an interpretation, but to be open to further evaluation and shifting and expanding interpretations. Dialectically speaking, no interpretation can be the absolute truth.

Note the following types of interpretations with suggestions on how to dialectically shift them.

Black and White Interpretations (Either/or; Dichotomous; All-or-Nothing Thinking): Language that signals this interpretation includes *always, never, every,* and *all the time,* among others. Black and white interpretations rarely see the whole picture and may negatively feed emotion mind. These interpretations lead to rigidity and inflexibility, the opposite of a dialectical orientation.

Dialectical Shift: If your interpretations seem extreme, think of opposite thoughts or beliefs, and then identify middle-ground ways of thinking. You may not believe the opposite thoughts or beliefs, but the intention is to practice flexibility in your interpretations.

Regret Orientation (Woulda, Coulda, Shoulda Thinking; or Hindsight Bias): A common idiom is "hindsight is 20/20." This means that past choices seem clear with the benefit of knowing all of the outcomes now. Regret orientation keeps you stuck in the past, rather than focusing on what you can do effectively right now.

Dialectical Shift: Rather than fixating on past mistakes, focus on what you can do to be effective in the present moment.

Mind-Reading: An assumption that you already know how others are thinking or feeling leads you to feel or act in a certain manner. None of us can read other peoples' minds.

Dialectical Shift: When you catch yourself mind-reading, check out your assumptions with other people, especially the person whose mind you are trying to read. The only way to know is to ask.

Minimization: Minimization happens when something large or significant is reduced to something very small. Sometimes this reduces the emotional impact of a situation (in the short-term), but the result is emotional invalidation.

Dialectical Shift: Observe and describe the situation accurately without adding or subtracting, validating your feelings.

Magnification: Magnification is the opposite of minimization. It happens when something that is small or insignificant is exaggerated into something that is very large. It is similar to looking at a kitten through a magnifying glass and seeing a tiger.

Dialectical Shift: As with minimization, observe and describe the situation accurately without adding or subtracting.

Catastrophizing: Catastrophizing is an extreme form of magnification. It involves taking a situation and continuing to build it and build it and build it in your mind into a calamity with dire consequences.

Dialectical Shift: Focus on the *one* situation or problem at hand without exaggerating it. Most situations do not end up with extreme and dire consequences, so take one thing at a time. Alternatively, purposefully catastrophize to the point of absurdity to break you out of this interpretation.

Fortune-Telling (Crystal Ball-Gazing): Fortune-telling interprets the future in negative ways, assuming that you already know what is going to happen.

Dialectical Shift: Rather than let a negative prediction of the future paralyze you, focus on what you can do effectively right now to cope with your situation or problem. Stay in the present moment.

Overgeneralization: Overgeneralization involves taking a small bit of information and applying it broadly across all kinds of different people and situations.

Dialectical Shift: Do not assume that your knowledge fits all people and all situations. Acknowledge when your information does fit, and actively look for times when it does not. Be open to not knowing all of the facts.

Selective Information-Gathering (Selective Abstraction; Mental Filter; or Confirmation Bias): Sometimes you gather information that fits with your current thought or belief, ignoring evidence to the contrary. Some other interpretations may be missing here.

Dialectical Shift: Actively gather information and viewpoints that are different from your own. Remember that you do not need to agree with these different perspectives, but that they may lead you to greater flexibility and more effective choices.

Labeling (Judging): Labeling reduces a person or situation to only a name. Labels fail to look at people and situations in a holistic manner and miss important subtleties or nuances.

Dialectical Shift: Let go of the urge to label a person or situation, as the world is usually more complex than labels and judging.

Personalization: Personalization makes it all about you. Frankly, most everything in the world is not about you.

Dialectical Shift: Remember that most of the time it is not about you. Take responsibility for what is yours and gently let go of the rest. Enjoy the ensuing freedom!

Emotion Mind "Reasoning": Emotion mind reasoning happens when emotion, and not reason, is the only filter for interpretations.

Dialectical Shift: Use mindfulness to move to Wise Mind and then re-evaluate.

Should Statements: These statements focus on judgments rather than the realities of a particular situation or interaction. Reality unfolds in ways that do not fit our preferences (i.e., what "should" happen).

Dialectical Shift: Focus on "what is," not what "should be." Stop "shoulding" on yourself and others.

Discounting Positives: The negatives and downsides of situations blind you to the positives. Minimizing or negating positives about yourself, others, situations, or the world is undialectical.

Dialectical Shift: Seek out positives, upsides, and silver linings for balance. Own the positives about yourself and give yourself credit. Seek the positives in people and situations that seem negative.

Blaming: Blaming makes everyone but you responsible for your problems and difficulties. Blaming relinquishes your power and control and leaves you dependent on others to fix a situation or your life.

Dialectical Shift: Someone or something else may be responsible for a problem, but your power and control comes from focusing on how you can influence situations and your life, if only through choosing how you respond.

Shifting and Expanding Interpretations Worksheet

Identify your current interpretation, thought, belief, or self-talk:

Identify the origins of this interpretation, thought, belief, or self-talk. Where did it come from and how could it have been useful at that time or in certain situations?

Describe how this interpretation, thought, belief, or self-talk is facilitating (or not facilitating) the attainment of your goals and/or what you want or need in the current situation.

What alternative interpretations, thoughts, beliefs, or self-talk are possible? Can you identify an expansion or shift?

Describe how these alternatives, expansions, or shifts might facilitate your goals and/or what you want or need in the current situation.

Continuum of Emotions

Emotions have different intensity levels. When we notice lower-intensity feelings, we can be proactive and more effective with skills use. If you struggle with intense emotions, use this chart to help you identify when those feelings happen at lower intensity levels, prompting you to use skills and your skills plans. With positive emotions, be mindful and appreciate them at all intensity levels, and be aware of the events and interpretations that create those feelings.

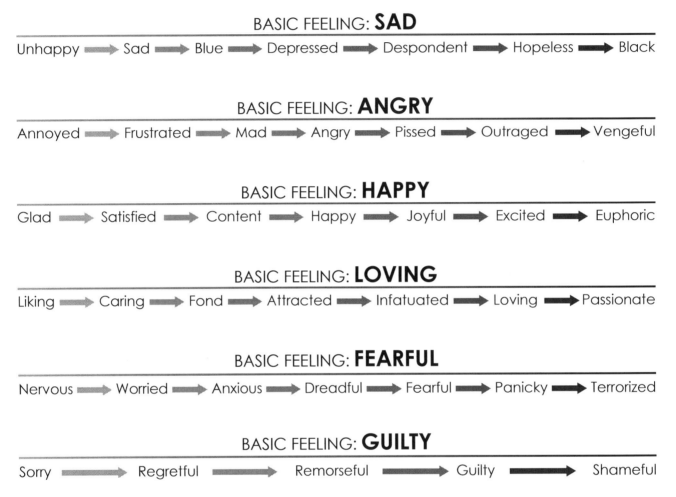

BASIC FEELING: **SAD**

Unhappy ➡ Sad ➡ Blue ➡ Depressed ➡ Despondent ➡ Hopeless ➡ Black

BASIC FEELING: **ANGRY**

Annoyed ➡ Frustrated ➡ Mad ➡ Angry ➡ Pissed ➡ Outraged ➡ Vengeful

BASIC FEELING: **HAPPY**

Glad ➡ Satisfied ➡ Content ➡ Happy ➡ Joyful ➡ Excited ➡ Euphoric

BASIC FEELING: **LOVING**

Liking ➡ Caring ➡ Fond ➡ Attracted ➡ Infatuated ➡ Loving ➡ Passionate

BASIC FEELING: **FEARFUL**

Nervous ➡ Worried ➡ Anxious ➡ Dreadful ➡ Fearful ➡ Panicky ➡ Terrorized

BASIC FEELING: **GUILTY**

Sorry ➡ Regretful ➡ Remorseful ➡ Guilty ➡ Shameful

If you have trouble identifying different feeling words, rate a basic emotion (e.g., depression, anxiety, or anger) on a continuum from 1 to 10 (low to high) or simply observe it as low, medium, or high. Then think about how to cope effectively with that emotion.

Changing How You Relate to Emotions

Emotions are not good, bad, right, or wrong. The first step to changing our relationship to feelings is to be curious about them and the messages they send to us.

Emotions motivate us in relationships and in other aspects of life. Emotions can be effective and can motivate behavior that has to happen automatically, without thought. A parent who chases a child into a busy street is motivated by emotion (i.e., fear), not by reason. Emotions enable us to overcome seemingly impossible obstacles at times.

Even when emotions seem to overtake life, such as when we are depressed or anxious or angry, it is important to remember that those emotions still give us important information. Rather than judging our emotions, practice acceptance of them and open your mind to their messages. Rejection of emotions or trying to push them away usually intensifies them. If the message is not heard, it needs to get louder. As an example, invalidation by others tends to intensify emotions, and self-invalidation has the same effect.

Practice nonjudgmental acceptance of your feelings and listen to their messages because trying to get rid of, fighting, or judging emotions unwittingly adds suffering to emotional pain. Willingness to be with your feelings soothes them. It is similar to hearing others' concerns and sitting with their distress without having to fix anything. *Not* fixing your feelings and being mindful of them is a solution, because even strong emotions do not require action.

Similar to Urge Surfing, we "hold" our emotions through mindfulness. Holding feelings means that you recognize them as a part of your experience, but not as who you are as a person. As you simply allow yourself to be with your emotions, you open yourself to their ebbs and flows and find that the intensity usually subsides.

Observe your emotions without getting stuck, and practice acceptance when they are painful. If you find yourself overwhelmed, change strategies and use distress tolerance skills.

You will find that emotions have important information for you, and they soothe themselves when you listen to them. Acceptance in the moment frees you from the grip your feelings have on you.

PLEASED ───────────────────────────────

Self-care goes by the wayside when struggling with mental illness and substance abuse, often because symptoms interfere with using these skills in the first place. Inadequate sleep, poor nutrition, a lack of exercise, and untreated medical issues result in emotional dysregulation that can cycle back into symptoms and chemical dependency. Just as a lack of self-care can cause or exacerbate problems, a concerted effort to increase self-care can alleviate them.

When people have neglected self-care in combination with abusing substances, they feel lousy. Because alcohol and drugs make people feel better in the short-term, feeling physically ill can be a trigger to continue the cycle of use. The way to break this cycle is to initiate balanced self-care while you practice other skills to manage your symptoms and urges.

Use the acronym **PLEASED** to remember the building blocks of this skill (**P**hysical Health, **L**ist Resources and Barriers, **E**at Balanced Meals, **A**void Drugs and Alcohol, **S**leep between 7 and 10 Hours, **E**xercise 20 to 60 Minutes, **D**aily). These building blocks are described in further detail in the paragraphs that follow.

Physical Health: Regular medical checkups and engaging in proactive skills and behaviors that keep our bodies healthy contribute to well-being. Treat physical illness when it arises and comply with medical advice. Take your medications as prescribed (or consult your prescriber), and make life changes to minimize use of medications when indicated. Always consider how your physical health impacts your mental health and urges to use.

List Resources and Barriers: Resources include skills we might already use (e.g., O2E, Pros and Cons, and Willingness), people who support us, and having knowledge about health and wellness. Identify strengths and all available resources for each part of the PLEASED skill. Barriers also abound with PLEASED skills. Develop a plan to use skills to address barriers.

Eat Balanced Meals: Eat three balanced meals plus a couple of healthy snacks mindfully throughout the day. Fruits, vegetables, whole grains, and lean protein are must-haves. Eat "whole" (unprocessed or minimally processed) or single-ingredient foods when possible. Drink 10 full glasses of water a day. Avoid eating too much or too little and minimize sugars, saturated fats, and food or beverages with little or no nutritional value. Replace "diets" with lifestyle changes and keep current on reputable nutritional information. Start small and build on success. Consult with a physician or nutritionist if needed. Remember that being overly hungry can trigger urges to use substances.

Avoid Drugs and Alcohol: As emphasized throughout this manual, the risks associated with drugs and alcohol, along with the emotional, physical, relational, financial, and other effects, can make their use problematic. If you find you need larger amounts to reach a "desired" effect and/or experience an inability to cut down or quit use, you need help and support.

Sleep between 7 and 10 Hours: Sleep is important to regulate your moods. Find an amount of sleep that works for you. See the instructions in the "Sleep Routine" section for more information.

Exercise 20 to 60 Minutes: Exercise for a minimum of 20 minutes three to five times weekly. Balanced exercise positively impacts symptoms of mental illness and decreases urges to use. Find natural ways of exercising, like taking stairs, parking at the far end of a parking lot, and playing with pets or children. Humans are not biologically designed to be sedentary, so movement is vital. Consult a physician with concerns about starting an exercise routine.

Daily: PLEASED skills need to be daily habits for you to reap their great benefits, but their positive effects cannot be overstated.

PLEASED Worksheet ────────────────

Improving our PLEASED skills significantly impacts how we feel and lowers our vulnerability to feeling negative and intense emotions. PLEASED skills also require daily attention and follow-through. Use the checklist spaces below to list your PLEASED behaviors for today, and be sure to check them off when they are completed. Notice how you feel before and after each PLEASED skill.

☐ _____

Distress/urge level before:_____ Distress/urge level after:_____

☐ _____

Distress/urge level before:_____ Distress/urge level after:_____

☐ _____

Distress/urge level before:_____ Distress/urge level after:_____

☐ _____

Distress/urge level before:_____ Distress/urge level after:_____

☐ _____

Distress/urge level before:_____ Distress/urge level after:_____

☐ _____

Distress/urge level before:_____ Distress/urge level after:_____

☐ _____

Distress/urge level before:_____ Distress/urge level after:_____

Sleep Routines

Behavioral interventions usually improve sleep over a period of a few weeks, and they may even work well enough to minimize or eliminate sleep medications for some people. The following suggestions will greatly improve your sleep if you practice them consistently, and they will probably be enjoyable, too.

- Create a sleep routine that begins at least one hour before going to bed. Like landing an airplane, healthy sleep involves getting into a pattern and getting the landing gear down well ahead of time. A sleep routine should consist of relaxing activities that cue the mind and body for sleep. Deep breathing, muscle relaxation, and mindfulness work well in a sleep routine.

- Establish consistent sleep and wake times. Avoid using the "snooze" button on your alarm clock.

- The bed should be for sleeping and intimacy only. Wakeful activities in bed confuse the mind and body, and the bed no longer becomes a cue for sleep and rest.

- Create a relaxing environment. A clean and uncluttered environment with fresh bed linens and comfortable blankets and pillows will help create the conditions for sleep. Also, block out sources of light and keep the temperature at a comfortable level, preferably a few degrees cooler than during the daytime.

- Avoid caffeine and nicotine for four hours (or more) before bedtime.

- Avoid heavy meals and spicy foods before bedtime.

- Avoid any stimulation before bedtime, including arguments or conflict, vigorous activity, or anything else that is likely to activate your mind and body.

- Get exercise during the daytime.

- Avoid daytime napping.

- If you are unable to sleep after 20 minutes, get up and do something boring and/or relaxing until you are sleepy and ready to return to bed.

List other ways to improve your sleep:

Build Mastery

Many of us have daily tasks that lead us to feel in control when completed. The flip side is that when these tasks build up, we tend to feel overwhelmed and out of control.

For example, basic activities of daily living (ADLs) need our daily attention. The following brief list includes basic Build Mastery activities for many of us:

- Hygiene (e.g., brushing teeth, cleaning self, wearing clean clothes)
- Doing the dishes
- Shopping for food and necessities
- Cleaning whatever needs it
- Doing laundry
- Following a to-do list
- Returning phone calls or emails
- Accomplishing important tasks or chores
- Opening mail and/or paying bills
- Completing homework or work tasks
- Tending to our children or pets
- Maintaining a certain level of organization
- Attending a meeting

In addition to ADLs, Build Mastery skills include taking on challenges and working toward goals. Here are some examples:

- Practicing DBT-S and relapse prevention skills
- Pursuing a hobby
- Initiating an exercise program
- Working on friendships
- Taking steps to resolve a problem
- Accomplishing tasks outside your comfort zone
- Dealing with an interpersonal issue
- Standing up for yourself
- Volunteering
- Doing your best in a tough situation
- Joining a club
- Staying sober today
- Learning something new

Technically, any attempt to be effective or any accomplishment can be considered to be a Build Mastery skill.

Be mindful of your efforts and give yourself due credit. Do not minimize or discount your attempts to build mastery. As a rule, if you would judge yourself when you have not made an effort or have not accomplished a task, then you deserve credit for the effort or accomplishment when you do try and when you get a task done.

Using Build Mastery skills decreases emotional vulnerability and increases our self-respect, leading to feeling better.

Build Mastery Worksheet ————————————

Certain activities and behaviors help us feel competent and in control (and overwhelmed and out-of-control when we neglect them). Build Mastery behaviors may vary day-to-day or week-to-week. Use the checklist spaces below to list your Build Mastery behaviors for today or this week, and be sure to check them off when they are completed. Notice how you feel before and after each accomplishment.

☐ _____

Distress/urge level before:_____ Distress/urge level after:_____

☐ _____

Distress/urge level before:_____ Distress/urge level after:_____

☐ _____

Distress/urge level before:_____ Distress/urge level after:_____

☐ _____

Distress/urge level before:_____ Distress/urge level after:_____

☐ _____

Distress/urge level before:_____ Distress/urge level after:_____

☐ _____

Distress/urge level before:_____ Distress/urge level after:_____

☐ _____

Distress/urge level before:_____ Distress/urge level after:_____

Build Positive Experience (BPE)

Emotions are a byproduct of what we think and what we do. Positive events and positive thoughts create positive feelings, but as straightforward as this concept seems, it can be difficult to put into action.

Symptoms of mental illness and barriers like lack of energy and motivation can discourage the occurrence of positive events, meaning that positive emotions remain unlikely. In these cases, use opposite action to get into Build Positive Experience. Interest, enjoyment, and energy will eventually follow positive events, especially if we invest in the experience without a strong desire or need to control the outcome. Let positive emotions happen organically.

As you work on abstinence, you may find that you have not developed many positive experiences that have not involved the use of alcohol and/or drugs. Your challenge now is to have good times without substances. It can and will happen if you coach and encourage yourself instead of imagining how much better it would be if you were high.

Sometimes we feel like we do not deserve positive experiences, we worry about expectations, or we dread positive experiences' ending. Treat these issues like distractions and mindfully re-focus on the positive experience. Other barriers to Build Positive Experience exist, too. Take a moment to consider barriers that apply to you.

Build Positive Experience includes positives that can happen right now as well as positives that can be planned in the short- and long-term future.

Positive Events Right Now: What can be a positive in the here and now or immediate future? Maybe it is a conversation, hearing or telling a joke, or helping someone. It might be taking a break, taking a quick walk, or taking a few minutes to practice mindfulness. You may find that the positive event is simply soaking in some sunshine, seeing rain wash everything clean, or feeling a warm breeze.

There are an enormous number of positive events possible now. We just need to turn our minds toward them and be open to the experience with our full attention. Read through the Activities List (p. 87) to find some possibilities.

Positive Events Planned in the Short Term: These positive events can include a regular family meal, an outing alone or with a friend, a Friday movie night, or anything you can plan and schedule over the short term.

List the interests, hobbies, and activities you like to do (or used to do) and add activities to try from the Activities List. If you have a short list, you may have to develop some additional interests through trying out a lot of new activities with an open mind. Plan time for these positive events in your schedule and follow through with them.

Short-term positive events need to be regular occurrences and planned daily to be effective. Having regular positive events that you look forward to and that you mindfully participate in moves you toward a satisfying life.

Positive Events to Work Toward in the Long Term: List your long-term priorities and goals. They may include going to school, learning a craft, making a career change, taking up an instrument, being in great physical shape, or having a vision for making a difference in the world. Of course, sobriety is an example of a long-term positive to work toward.

Pick something from your list and break it down into manageable steps. Plan and schedule time to work on that first step, and follow through on it. As you accomplish each step, give yourself credit and plan and schedule the next step. All great journeys unfold one step at a time.

Your work toward long-term positives is a major part of building a satisfying life. Remember that some steps can be hard or frustrating. Do not give up, and stay focused on your long term goals.

Positive Event Planning, Scheduling, and Your Routine: You may not know what to do to build or plan positive experiences. As stated earlier, first, you should identify possible positive experiences and schedule them, or they are less likely to happen. Then you have to follow through with your plan using Opposite to Emotion when needed.

Mindfulness and Positive Events: Using Build Positive Experience requires you to bring your Mindfulness skills along. When distractions occur, gently notice and release them, and then refocus on your BPE.

Build Positive Experience Worksheet ————

Identify at least one BPE for each day this week, including the details of where and when you will participate in those experiences. Also record your distress and/or urge levels before and after the mindful participation in each BPE. Notice how BPE tends to be beneficial to improving emotions and managing urges. Check off the completion of your daily BPEs.

☐ **MONDAY** BPE _____ When & Where_____

Distress/urge level before:_____ Distress/urge level after:_____

☐ **TUESDAY** BPE _____ When & Where_____

Distress/urge level before:_____ Distress/urge level after:_____

☐ **WEDNESDAY** BPE _____ When & Where_____

Distress/urge level before:_____ Distress/urge level after:_____

☐ **THURSDAY** BPE _____ When & Where_____

Distress/urge level before:_____ Distress/urge level after:_____

☐ **FRIDAY** BPE _____ When & Where_____

Distress/urge level before:_____ Distress/urge level after:_____

☐ **SATURDAY** BPE _____ When & Where_____

Distress/urge level before:_____ Distress/urge level after:_____

☐ **SUNDAY** BPE _____ When & Where_____

Distress/urge level before:_____ Distress/urge level after:_____

Attend to Relationships (A2R)

Symptoms of mental illness, substance use, and their associated behaviors can disrupt relationships. You may have neglected friends and family or have simply lost track of those connections. At other times, you may have actively damaged relationships or burned out others with your problems. You may feel lonely, and isolation tends to create and maintain unwanted feelings.

Attending to Relationships is a form of Build Positive Experience that creates positive feelings over time through investing in and enjoying people who are important to you.

Start with two lists of people: those who are currently in your life and those from the past who you would want in your life again. Only list people with whom you have or had a positive connection with overall. *Do not list unhealthy people or people with whom you have had hopeless relationships. Also avoid people who have encouraged you to participate in unhealthy behaviors like using substances.*

People I would like to have a better relationship with:

Specific steps I can take to improve these relationships:

People I would like to reconnect with:

Specific steps I can take to reconnect with these people:

Mood Momentum (MM)

We influence feelings with the behaviors we choose. When we experience an emotion that we want to continue, we can use Mood Momentum. This skill directs us to stay involved in events and thoughts that maintain our positive emotions so we can benefit from the momentum of already feeling good. This skill is especially beneficial for people who use substances to continue "feeling good" or riding an otherwise natural high.

Emotions tend naturally to draw us to behaviors that are congruent or fit with them. Mood Momentum is a mindful effort to choose healthy mood-congruent behaviors when they will be helpful. Ways to continue positive moods include the following:

Engage in using Build Positive Experience

Balance using BPE with using Build Mastery

Use mindfulness to reflect on a positive emotion

Engage in using PLEASED

Balance active positive events with relaxing positive events

Engage in healthy relationships

Work on a responsibility and stay mindful of your efforts and accomplishments (and avoid judgments)

Practice mindfulness exercises

Work on a hobby or project or try something on the Activities List

Think of other ways you can use Mood Momentum:

A key to Mood Momentum is to pick from a variety of positive experiences, activities, and behaviors to keep it interesting. Even the most fun or relaxing event will eventually reach the point where it no longer creates a positive effect. We benefit most from MM when we take a balanced approach, switch up our strategies, and keep it fresh.

If you have tried to maintain positive moods through substance use, remember that this skill can be used to replace substance use behaviors in order to continue feeling good in a way that does not compromise your mental health and sobriety.

Opposite to Emotion (O2E)

We get stuck in difficult emotions due in part to mood-congruent behavior. Mood-congruent behavior occurs when we fall into behavior patterns that keep our negative emotions around. For example, when we feel depressed, we may respond by:

- Becoming isolated (e.g., being disconnected from relationships, not answering the phone, missing social engagements and appointments)

- Being inactive (e.g., staying in bed or on the couch, not participating in hobbies or potentially positive experiences, letting chores and other responsibilities pile up)

- Engaging in stuck thinking (e.g., focusing only on the negative, ruminating, wanting to die)

- Neglecting self-care and hygiene

- Eating and sleeping too much or too little

- Deciding to stop therapy and medications

- Engaging in other behaviors that perpetuate negative emotional states

Unfortunately, these reactions to depression keep us depressed and may even make it worse. This is where Opposite to Emotion (also known as Opposite Action) helps. This dialectical skill directs us to act in ways that are the opposite of the behaviors our difficult emotions pull us toward. For the depressive examples above, we would use Opposite to Emotion to:

- Reach out to relationships for assistance and positive experience.

- Get moving by doing activities, hobbies, and important tasks.

- Practice dialectical thinking, take a nonjudgmental stance, or use Encouragement.

- Use PLEASED.

- Go to therapy appointments and discuss medication issues with your prescriber before making sudden changes on your own.

See the following explanations and examples for ways to use Opposite Action to address common difficult emotions.

Opposite to Emotion with Anxiety or Fear: Anxiety and fear lead to avoidance, and avoidance gets reinforced because it protects us from distress in the short-term. However, the more we avoid, the more our anxieties build over time, and the more overwhelmed we end up feeling.

Using Opposite Action means approaching anxieties and fears one step at a time and learning to tolerate the distress that comes with it. The key is to start small and gradually build up to larger fears. The more we approach rather than avoid, the more our nervous system learns to be "bored," and the less anxious we feel.

We can also learn to accept our anxious thoughts and sensations rather than judge them, fight them, or catastrophize about them. This acceptance-based approach takes the power out of anxieties and has the paradoxical effect of them diminishing them.

Opposite to Emotion with Anger: Anger leads to replaying anger-inducing situations over and over in our minds as well as coming across to others as hostile and sometimes lashing out. It also may include self-harming behaviors or contribute to difficulties maintaining sobriety. Many people find that harboring resentments is a primary factor in continuing to use and in relapse.

Using Opposite Action means being kind and compassionate to others and yourself. We can spend quality time with our pets and children, being careful to be gentle and not to displace our anger, and we can choose to do something to soothe or take care of ourselves.

Alternatively, we might imagine compassion for someone we feel anger toward. If you are angry at yourself, remember that you also need self-compassion. Most people, including you, do not want to make mistakes and do not want others to be angry at them, no matter how unskillfully they act. Compassion can be dialectically balanced with accountability.

Distract from angry thoughts by using the Thoughts skill. Count to 10 or recite the alphabet. Focus on thoughts that are the opposite of angry thoughts.

Do not stuff anger, because this sets the stage for rage. When anger is at a workable level, see if it fits Wise Mind and use Interpersonal Effectiveness skills if needed.

Opposite to Emotion with Guilt and Shame: We feel guilt when we have done something to hurt ourselves or others or when we make mistakes. Often we try to avoid or hide from others when we feel guilt, or we try to blame or otherwise avoid accepting responsibility for our actions. *Not making amends is a set-up to falling back into problem behavior.*

Using Opposite Action means addressing what happened with whomever was affected. Apologize and try to make the situation better if possible. If the situation cannot be improved, then try to do something better somewhere; this is a symbolic way to "right" a "wrong." Be committed to not repeating the same mistakes and develop a plan to act differently in the future.

A genuine apology is to assuage the other person and not a means for avoiding consequences. Others may continue to be upset for a time after an apology. Be patient with the process. Accept consequences with grace unless they do not fit the situation as evaluated in Wise Mind. Do not participate in guilt or consequences that are out of proportion with the situation.

After you have completed the steps listed here, let go of the situation and the thoughts that caused the guilt. Use Radical Acceptance.

If you feel guilty because of a SLIP, repair the mistake(s) if you are able and get back to your skills and action plan(s) to reduce the impact of emotions that will keep you in a cycle of substance use. Sometimes Wise Mind does not accept guilt. For example, we have a right to say no and to have boundaries, and we do not need to feel guilty for exerting this right. We may experience guilt in the absence of wrongdoing for a variety of reasons. Examples include feeling guilty for practicing Self-Soothe skills, for having a good time, or for taking time for ourselves. This type of guilt leads us to avoid behaviors like saying no, setting boundaries, and participating in beneficial activities.

When we have guilt that Wise Mind does not endorse, the Opposite Action is to approach rather than to avoid. Keep practicing saying no, setting boundaries, and participating in activities until you no longer feel guilt as a response. Remember to encourage yourself to overcome this type of guilt and to use a non-judgmental stance.

We feel shame when guilt is not addressed, when we have done something serious, or when something serious has happened to us. Shame can involve having judgments about being damaged, unlovable, or unforgivable.

We can also feel shame for how we look or who we are as people even when it does not fit Wise Mind. This type of shame frequently originates from others' judgments and from being mistreated. Shame causes us to hide, and hiding keeps the shame around.

Using Opposite Action with shame involves coming out of hiding and talking about what causes us shame with someone *safe, nonjudgmental, and accepting.* As we work through shame, we can open ourselves up to more and more supportive people and begin to heal. The process of working through shame also requires a nonjudgmental stance and Distress Tolerance skills.

O2E with Urges to Use: U-Turn

A u-turn means making a complete change of direction. Sometimes urges to use lead us to take steps to make substance use happen, leading to a relapse. Imagine a continuum where one direction leads to greater health and well-being and the other direction leads to diminished health and well-being. Sometimes we get moving in an ineffective direction (accidently or by choice), but once we realize we are moving farther away from our goals, we can make an abrupt change and head in the other direction.

Think about times when you have been driving or been a passenger in a car that has taken a wrong turn and is moving away from the destination. How does it feel to willfully stay on this route in spite of increasing indications that the direction is leading to a place you do not want to go? The reality is that it is possible to stop, re-assess the situation, and make a u-turn if needed, and that many opportunities to turn around usually exist until we have actually acted on an urge. Even if you have a lapse, there is still an opportunity to turn it around by recognizing the mistake, quickly repairing it, and reversing course before a full-blown relapse happens.

When we understand the vulnerabilities and triggers that lead to substance use, we can identify many intersections in which to make a u-turn and avoid being in a place that we want to avoid. The next time you notice urges and behaviors that move you toward relapse, take the wheel and make a u-turn.

O2E/U-Turn Worksheet

EVENT → **EMOTION/URGE** → **NATURAL RESPONSE**

FOLLOWED NATURAL RESPONSE?

YES

NO

ACTION

OPPOSITE ACTION

OUTCOMES

OUTCOMES

Interpersonal Effectiveness Module

Interpersonal effectiveness has three sets of skills that meet three different goals. Used together, these sets of skills improve our ability to interact with all types of people and to have more effective relationships.

The first set of these skills is FAST. FAST is about self-respect, and it is designed for you to live in a way that emphasizes fairness, truthfulness, and values. When we live according to our values, we develop a solid core of identity and feel good about ourselves and our choices. When you have a healthy relationship with yourself, then you have better relationships with others.

The second set of skills is GIVE. These skills teach us to show interest in others and to respond to them in a genuine manner, emphasizing understanding their experience and being able to validate it. GIVE skills also assist us in conflict resolution.

The last set of interpersonal effective skills is DEAR MAN. DEAR MAN is a model of assertiveness, used to increase the probability that you will get your wants and needs met. DEAR MAN is also used to empower you to say no when needed (like when refusing substances) and to set healthy boundaries.

Interpersonal Effectiveness and Dialectics

Balance is central to maintaining healthy relationships. Being too focused either on ourselves or others leads to unmet wants and needs and conflict. Instead, it is desirable to find middle ground in relationships, depending on the interaction and the context of what is needed.

Think of GIVE and DEAR MAN existing on a dialectic:

At times we need to focus on others and at other times we need to focus on ourselves. In practice, we are most effective when we blend both sets of skills. The blend between thinking about others versus ourselves is grounded in FAST. We use our values to guide us in relationships to enhance our self-respect and others' respect for us.

Ask yourself three questions when working the dialectic in relationships:

What does the other person need in this interaction (GIVE)?

What do I need in this interaction (DEAR MAN)?

What is needed in this interaction to maintain or build my self-respect (FAST)?

FAST (F)

FAST skills are focused on our priorities, goals, and values so we can make choices that build our self-respect. Self-respect is the foundation to liking ourselves, and it creates a solid base for us to build and maintain relationships with others.

Use the acronym FAST to remember the building blocks of this skill (Fair, Apologies Not Needed, Stick to Values, Truth and Accountability). These building blocks are described in further detail in the paragraphs that follow.

Fair: Be just and take a nonjudgmental stance with yourself and others. Avoid extremes and ground yourself in Wise Mind in interactions with others. Think of fair weather as being neither too hot nor too cold and without storms. Keep a moderate climate with others without whipping up bad weather. Use respectful words and actions with yourself and others. Others do *not* need to earn your respect. We treat others with respect because it builds our own self-worth. *Respond rather than react in relationships.*

Apologies Not Needed: Do not engage in unneeded apologetic behavior. Do not apologize for having an opinion or for your own viewpoints. You are allowed to disagree. Do not apologize for being you. Avoid apologies for things over which you have no control. Chronic, unnecessary apologies erode self-respect and devalue apologies that are genuinely needed. Note that "no apologies" does not apply to situations that require an apology (e.g., hurting someone).

Stick to Values: Use your priorities, goals, and values as guides and ground yourself in them. Choose behaviors and have interactions with others that build your self-respect. Identify what is important to you and stick to it. Know what values are non-negotiable, and when values conflict, work to resolve the conflict through Wise Mind. Live your true intentions based on your values.

Truth and Accountability: Be honest and accountable with yourself and others. Sometimes we avoid the truth because we are afraid of the consequences, but trying to deceive others destroys self-respect and can cause greater problems. Even if you have a great memory and can keep from getting tangled in a web of lies, *you* will still know the truth. Being accountable is more effective in most cases.

When dealing with substance use, lying and keeping secrets will almost always increase the negative effects on emotions, others, and your life in general. *Lying and keeping secrets keeps the doors to substance use cracked open, and most experts agree that being less than 100% truthful about your urges, thoughts, and plans to use is a sure route to relapse.*

In addition, act in a manner that respects your true abilities and avoid feigned helplessness and excuses. Take responsibility for yourself.

Values Inventory

This is a partial list of values. You might have an important value that is not on the list or notice some overlap between values. Review the list and circle your top ten values. Use your selected values in the exercises that follow.

Acceptance	Commitment	Effectiveness
Achievement	Compassion	Empathy
Activity	Confidence	Encouragement
Adaptability	Connection	Endurance
Adventurousness	Consistency	Energy
Affectionateness	Contentment	Enjoyment
Altruism	Contribution	Enthusiasm
Ambition	Cooperation	Excellence
Assertiveness	Courage	Exploration
Attentiveness	Courteousness	Expressiveness
Availability	Creativity	Fairness
Awareness	Credibility	Faith
Balance	Decisiveness	Family
Belongingness	Dependability	Fellowship
Bravery	Determination	Fidelity
Calm	Devotion	Financial independence
Capability	Dignity	Firmness
Caring	Discipline	Fitness
Challenge	Discretion	Freedom
Charity	Diversity	Friendship
Cleanliness	Drive	Fun
Closeness	Duty	Generosity
Comfort	Education	Giving

Grace	Neatness	Self-reliance
Gratitude	Openness	Sensitivity
Happiness	Optimism	Service
Harmony	Order	Sharing
Health	Passion	Simplicity
Honesty	Peace	Sincerity
Honor	Persistence	Sobriety
Hopefulness	Playfulness	Spirituality
Humility	Pleasantness	Spontaneity
Humor	Pleasure	Stability
Hygiene	Popularity	Strength
Imagination	Practicality	Structure
Independence	Pragmatism	Success
Integrity	Privacy	Support
Intelligence	Professionalism	Teamwork
Intensity	Prosperity	Thankfulness
Intimacy	Recovery	Thoughtfulness
Joy	Relaxation	Trust
Kindness	Reliability	Truth
Knowledge	Religion	Usefulness
Leadership	Resilience	Warmth
Learning	Resoluteness	Willingness
Love	Respect	Wisdom
Loyalty	Restraint	
Mindfulness	Sacrifice	
Modesty	Security	
Motivation	Self-control	

Once your values are identified, you can describe specific behaviors that you can practice to live your values with intention. The following are examples for how you can complete this exercise:

I value: *TRUTH*

Describe three specific ways you can live this value:

Be honest when others ask how I'm doing

Report when I have had a SLIP so I can learn from it

Take responsibility for mistakes that I make

I value: *FRIENDSHIP*

Describe three specific ways you can live this value:

Return phone calls from my friends

Listen and be supportive of other people in meetings

Practice "give and take" in my relationships

I value: *PEACE*

Describe three specific ways you can live this value:

Not yell at my wife and kids when I am angry

Practice MINDFULNESS exercises in the morning and at bedtime

Use acceptance and stop judging myself

I value: *HEALTH*

Describe three specific ways you can live this value:

Practice my PLEASED skills

Use opposite to emotion when depressed or anxious

Work hard to eliminate drugs and alcohol

Now it's your turn:

I value:

Describe three specific ways you can live this value:

I value:

Describe three specific ways you can live this value:

I value:

Describe three specific ways you can live this value:

I value:

Describe three specific ways you can live this value:

I value:

Describe three specific ways you can live this value:

I value:

Describe three specific ways you can live this value:

I value:

Describe three specific ways you can live this value:

I value:

Describe three specific ways you can live this value:

Values Conflict Worksheet ————————————

Our values frequently come into conflict, and we need to find ways to resolve those tensions in different situations. To move toward resolution, try to decide what your highest ranking values and priorities are and what will best meet the demands of the situation. The overall goal is to maintain and build self-respect. Choices that maintain and build self-respect may mean committing to difficult decisions and actions in some cases. Use Wise Mind to consider the short- and long-term results of each potential course of action. This exercise can also be helpful when you are struggling to maintain mental health and sobriety.

The following exercise will help you resolve value conflicts.

Describe the situation non-judgmentally:

Describe the priorities, goals, and values in conflict:

Rank the priorities, goals, and values from most to least important:

Describe options that either honor your top-ranked value(s) or that show adequate respect across values:

Evaluate the options. Describe a course of action from Wise Mind that maintains or builds self-respect:

Note: Occasionally we must make choices that sacrifice important values. Make these decisions from Wise Mind and only when the outcome is essential.

GIVE (G)

GIVE skills focus on others. Relationships work best when our wants, needs, and desires stay in balance with those of the people around us. Everyone benefits from relationships grounded in genuine interest and validation, and healthy relationships are essential to maintaining mental health and recovery. GIVE is also key to resolving conflicts.

Use the acronym GIVE to remember the building blocks of this skill (Genuine, Interested, Validate, Easy Manner). These building blocks are described in further detail in the paragraphs that follow.

Genuine: Be honest, sincere, and real with others. Speak and act from your heart with caring and use mindfulness to be with others in the moment. Let others know that you value them and treat them with respect. Recognize and address how substance use and/or sobriety affect your ability to be genuine in relationships.

Interested: Interest comes from efforts to connect with a person. Let others have the focus. Listen intently to others and pause to make space before responding. Ask questions and listen to the answers.

Be mindful of your nonverbal communication. Our nonverbals communicate a great deal of information to others, both intentionally and unintentionally. Send the nonverbal messages that you want to send to others. Nonverbally, interest is communicated by looking at the person, making appropriate eye contact, and keeping your mannerisms and posture open and relaxed.

Validate: To validate means to acknowledge others' feelings, thoughts, beliefs, and experience non-judgmentally. Validation is "walking a mile in others' shoes," and seeing life from their perspective. We validate when we find others' truths and how their experiences make sense given their life circumstances and the situation. (See VALIDATE) *Remember to validate yourself, too.*

Easy Manner: Remember the idiom: "You catch more flies with honey than with vinegar." Having an easy manner means treating others with kindness and a relaxed attitude. It also means not being heavy-handed with our judgments, opinions, and viewpoints. Allow space for others.

We can always raise our interpersonal intensity if necessary. It can be more effective to start out in a relatively relaxed and laid-back manner.

VALIDATION (V)

Validation is a complicated skill. Use this expanded teaching to learn a more advanced approach to this GIVE building block.

Use the acronym **VALIDATE** to remember the building blocks of this skill (Value Others, Ask Questions, Listen and Reflect, Identify with Others, Discuss Emotions, Attend to Nonverbals, Turn the Mind, Encourage Participation). These building blocks are described in further detail in the paragraphs that follow.

Value Others: Seeking the inherent value in others is essential to validation. Adopt an attitude of acceptance toward others. Demonstrate your caring and concern, and let others know they are important to you.

Ask Questions: We ask questions to help clarify others' experience. Ask specific questions about what others are feeling as well as about thoughts and beliefs. Ask questions to make sure you understand accurately. Be genuinely curious about what is behind behaviors. Use questions to draw out others' experience.

Listen and Reflect: Listen to others' answers to your questions and reflect back the major themes. Invite others to confirm your understanding (or lack of understanding). Continue to question, listen, and reflect for clarity.

Identify with Others: Work to see the world through the eyes of others. How do relationships and the world make sense to *them*? Seek to understand others, identifying when you can and accepting differences when you cannot.

Discuss Emotions: Talk about others' feelings and how they affect them from *their* perspective (not how they affect you). Acknowledging the impact of others' experience on them demonstrates understanding.

Attend to Nonverbals: Notice others' nonverbal communication to give you information about their experience. Do they look open or closed? Are they making eye contact? Read facial expressions and body language to identify feelings, and then check out your observations with others for accuracy.

Turn the Mind: Validation does not mean that we agree with others. Validation means that we non-judgmentally accept what they feel, think, and experience and how their behaviors make sense given their context. Turn the mind toward validation, especially when it is difficult to relate to an individual. Turning the mind is especially important in conflicts.

Encourage Participation: Validation can be a difficult process at times, so we need to encourage ourselves and others to be engaged with each other. Do not give up, even when understanding is hard, when you feel disconnected, or when you are in conflict with others.

DEAR MAN (DM)

The DEAR MAN skill focuses on us. We use DEAR MAN to get our wants and needs met, to say no, and to set boundaries. This skill is the DBT version of assertiveness. *Clearly and proactively communicating your wants and needs to others is vitally important to maintaining mental health and recovery.*

The building blocks of DEAR MAN (described later in this section) work best together, but some of them can be used independently (e.g., you can assert without using any other DEAR MAN building blocks). Use as much or as little of DEAR MAN as is required by the situation. To be most effective, approach DEAR MAN with the following core assumptions and guidelines:

Others cannot read your mind: This includes your closest friends and family. Assume that others are oblivious and cannot tell how you are feeling or know what you want or need; it may feel personal but it is simply reality. We sometimes get frustrated and blame others when our wants and needs go unmet. We need to *ask* for our wants and needs, say *no* when appropriate, and *maintain* our own boundaries.

Effective communication of your wants and needs requires words: Do not sigh, sulk, cop an attitude, get destructive, withdraw, or otherwise communicate without thoughtful words *and* expect it to work effectively. It is true that our behaviors communicate volumes–just not clearly.

DEAR MAN does not always work, even when done effectively: DEAR MAN increases the probability that you will get your wants and needs met, but it does not guarantee it. Sometimes self-respect (e.g., that you spoke up or tried) is the consolation prize.

You must be mindful of your DEAR MAN goals before you begin: Decide what is important and what is negotiable before you use DEAR MAN.

Remember to balance DEAR MAN with GIVE grounded in FAST: Attending to others (GIVE) makes them more willing to assist, accept when you say no, and respect your boundaries. Keep track of priorities, goals, and values in relationships (FAST).

By learning and practicing assertiveness, you can avoid and prevent resentments: All of us require some of our wants and needs to be met to feel good about the people in our lives. Similarly, we need to learn how to say no and set boundaries to avoid feeling like a door mat and used by others. Part of avoiding resentments is speaking up.

Use the acronym **DEAR MAN** to remember the building blocks of this skill (Describe, Express, Assert, Reward, Mindful, Appear Confident, Negotiate). These building blocks are described in further detail in the paragraphs that follow.

Describe: Use observe and describe to outline the situation in nonjudgmental language. Identify the facts that will support your request, your reason for saying no, or your need for a boundary.

Express: Share your opinions and feelings if they relate and will help others to understand the situation. Sometimes you may choose not to include this step.

Assert: Ask clearly for what you want or need, say no, or set your boundary. Establish your DEAR MAN goals up front so you know what you want out of the situation and work to be straightforward and matter of fact. The assert step is essential. Otherwise, no one will know what you want or need.

Reward: Let others know what is in it for them. How will meeting your wants and needs, accepting your refusal, or respecting your boundaries benefit the relationship? Try to focus on rewards rather than threats. Create opportunities for others to feel positive about helping or respecting for you. However, sometimes we need to discuss consequences instead of rewards. Again, be matter of fact, and avoid ultimatums that will box everyone in. Overall, try to provide incentives to others for meeting your wants and needs.

Mindful: Use a "broken record" approach. Others will often try to change the subject or throw in comments to derail you. Repeat your request or limits over and over again, but also be aware of when the broken record technique is not working and switch strategies accordingly.

Appear Confident: Act as if you feel confident even if you do not. Pretend you have the confidence you have seen in someone else. Use an assertive tone of voice, make eye contact, and use confident body language. Be mindful of your facial expression (keeping it relatively neutral) as well as your posture and overall personal appearance. Use nonverbal communication to your advantage. Write down and practice your DEAR MAN skills before using them so you feel more confident in the actual situation.

Negotiate: Negotiation means that we compromise and are willing to give to get. Decide what compromises make sense if you cannot meet your desired DEAR MAN goal(s). If you get stuck, turn the issue over to the other person for options to solve it; for example, say, "What do you think will work?" Turning the tables shifts the dialectical balance and can get the process moving again.

Negotiation is a dialectical strategy to get wants and needs met by meeting someplace in the middle. However, in some cases, you may decide in Wise Mind that negotiation is not an option.

DEAR MAN Factors to Consider

Be in Wise Mind: Wise Mind is essential for the effective use of DEAR MAN. If you are not in Wise Mind, consider soothing your emotions before using DEAR MAN in most cases. (Sometimes using DEAR MAN based in emotion mind is needed; e.g., if safety is an immediate issue.)

Use GIVE First: Start an interaction with GIVE to increase your effectiveness. Others are more receptive when you consider their feelings, point of view, and situation. GIVE can open doors for using DEAR MAN.

Think About Timing: It's been said that "timing is everything." They also say, "There's no time like the present." Both of these sayings have truth. Consider whether the timing of your use of DEAR MAN seems to favor it, but do not use timing as an excuse to put off using DEAR MAN when you need to, especially if the situation is time sensitive.

Direct DEAR MAN Appropriately: Make sure you speak to someone who can actually respond to your use of DEAR MAN. Sometimes it is difficult to predict if someone will respond well to your use of DEAR MAN. Start where you can and be respectful at all times, then move on to a different person if your use of DEAR MAN is not working. Remember that even if one person may not be able to help you when you use DEAR MAN, he or she might have influence with the next person you address.

Do Not Give Up: DEAR MAN is a difficult skill that varies in its effectiveness. Practice it in everyday situations and you will improve your overall assertiveness.

Interpersonal Intensity (II)

Effective use of DEAR MAN sometimes depends on our level of intensity. Assertiveness is a dialectical concept, with passivity on one end and aggressiveness on the other:

PASSIVE ⟷ **ASSERTIVE** ⟷ **AGGRESSIVE**

There are times to be more passive or more aggressive, but the most effective level of assertiveness is usually someplace in the middle. When we are too passive, it is easy for others to dismiss us, but when we are too aggressive, others get defensive and resist our demands. Use observe and describe to make a Wise Mind assessment of each unique situation.

It works to start in the low-middle end of the dialectic in most situations. From the low-middle end, you can dial up the intensity if needed; it is less effective to start out too intense and then try to dial it down.

Consider your baseline interpersonal style when applying Interpersonal Intensity. If you are normally passive, an effective DEAR MAN level will probably feel uncomfortably aggressive. If you are normally aggressive, an effective DEAR MAN level will probably feel uncomfortably passive. Closely observe others' reactions and responsiveness and adjust your Interpersonal Intensity accordingly.

Sometimes it is hard to gauge if you are being passive, assertive, or aggressive. Consider the following descriptions to guide you:

Qualities of being passive: You struggle to say no and easily (or automatically) give in to others' requests, even when you do not want to. You have trouble setting boundaries and standing up for your rights, and you avoid conflict at all costs.

Qualities of being assertive: You are direct, speaking confidently and maintaining eye contact. You are able to express your wants and needs without having to "beat around the bush" and can say and stick to "no." You are able to take responsibility for yourself, and you act in a respectful and thoughtful manner in resolving conflicts.

Qualities of being aggressive: You are focused on having things your way, no matter the effect on others. You interact with a loud, forceful, and argumentative style. You can be prone to bullying others into doing what you want, and you are not shy about initiating conflicts, taking a "win at all costs" approach.

To practice adjusting your interpersonal level of intensity, do behavioral rehearsal responding to different situations at different levels, followed by discussion on what was most effective.

DEAR MAN Bill of Rights

Review the bill of rights below. Refer to it to encourage yourself to use DEAR MAN. Also, remember that rights require responsibility, so use DEAR MAN mindfully and effectively. Choose your "DEAR MAN" moments wisely.

- I have the right to be treated with respect.

- I have the right to my own opinions.

- I have the right to express my feelings.

- I have the right to stand up for my values.

- I have the right to disagree with others.

- I have the right to understand a request before agreeing.

- I have the right to ask for information.

- I have the right to take time to think about a request.

- I have the right to say no without guilt.

- I have the right to ask for my wants and needs.

- I have the right to set healthy boundaries with others.

- I have the right to be in Wise Mind before I get into a discussion.

- I have the right to disengage from a conflict.

- I have other rights related to my needs and wants.

List other DEAR MAN rights:

Conflict Resolution

Many of us have conflicts with others (or may avoid them at all costs). Use the following steps to guide you through conflicts. As with other interpersonal skills, it is essential to do behavioral rehearsal with your therapist, program members, or someone else, especially if you struggle with handling conflict effectively.

- Address issues proactively with DEAR MAN to keep the potential for and intensity of conflicts lower.

- When in conflict, step back and see if you and others are in Wise Mind. If you want to win or be "right" more than seek understanding and resolution, you are probably not in Wise Mind. Emotion mind conflicts are rarely effective. If either of you are not in Wise Mind, disengage and discuss the issue later. Use distress tolerance skills before getting back into the issue(s).

- Consider the relevant issues. Use Wise Mind to consider whether this is a conflict worth having right now with this person. Consider your priorities, goals, values, and the nature of the conflict. Pick your conflicts wisely.

- Use FAST throughout any interpersonal situation and especially with conflict. Lowering yourself to another's "level" will decrease your self-respect and will rarely result in an effective outcome.

- Start with GIVE. Think about companies with great customer service. They avoid arguing and listen instead and then let you know they understand your problem. This approach frequently defuses arguments.

- Use a non-judgmental stance and you might find that you agree with at least some of what the other person has to say. Breathe and give some space before you respond. Many conflicts escalate because of a mutual lack of listening coupled with rapid-fire responses.

- Use DEAR MAN effectively. Be clear about your wants and needs, saying no, or setting boundaries. Do so in a matter-of-fact way without calling names, labeling, judging, or getting into extremes.

- Use Radical Acceptance when conflicts are not resolved or when others are upset and angry. Not all conflicts have an immediate resolution. Sometimes we need to step away and let it be. When resolution seems unlikely or when the conflict is escalating, gently disengage yourself and agree to revisit it later.

- Remember that negotiation and making Wise Mind concessions are useful. Stay away from all-or-nothing in situations and work the dialectic.

- Do not engage in conflicts when under the influence of substances. Substance use dramatically decreases the probability that the conflict will be handled respectfully and skillfully, and it dramatically increases the probability that the conflict will escalate.

Using DEAR MAN to Refuse Substances

When people give up substances (or are working to do so) it is common to encounter pressures, both subtle and obvious, to take up using again. You may find yourself in situations where others are drinking and/or using drugs and where it seems to be part of the "norm." In these situations you may find that others encourage you to use, sometimes in seemingly friendly ways, and sometimes in pushy ways. Sometimes the encouragement is subtle, being passive and implied.

In situations where you are offered alcohol, drugs, or anything else that is unwanted, you can simply say "no" without any additional information or justifications. Saying no is difficult for many people. For this reason, it is important to do behavior rehearsal, having your therapist, a fellow program member, or someone else "pressure" you to use while you practice setting a limit. Have your behavior rehearsal partner continue to challenge you in more intense ways while you continue to use broken record. Note that you can also rehearse other ways of refusing if you find that to be useful.

As you rehearse this skill, remember to practice different scenarios (e.g., being at a social event, having someone bring substances to your home, having your partner or spouse encourage you to use with him/her) with different people (e.g., strangers, a close friend, a family member), making the rehearsal as real as possible. It helps to have people share actual events with each other to increase the realism of the rehearsal. Having one or more observers to give feedback and to "jump into" the rehearsal to model skills when you get stuck increases the effectiveness of this exercise. Writing a script to follow can assist those who are in the process learning how to speak more spontaneously.

Remember that you have worked hard for your successes, and people who would ridicule, criticize, or pressure someone who has worked to improve have their own issues. Try not to personalize, and remember that you can simply leave the situation if necessary. Use your Wise and Clear Mind to guide you.

Using Interpersonal Effectiveness to Address Resentments

Resentments contribute to painful emotions, substance use, and other ineffective behaviors. Start by observing and describing the role resentments have had in your life with your therapist and/or program members. We can be surprised how much resentment we have once we begin to talk about it. In these discussions, be straightforward in how you have played a role in and participated in resentments.

Resentments can then be divided into categories. One category is for resentments that you decide to accept and release without addressing them with other people, essentially beginning a process of unburdening yourself. It is helpful to share your desire to release these resentments with someone else, and you may find that you need to revisit this process of acceptance from time to time.

The other category is for resentments that need to be addressed with other people, directly or symbolically. Begin by talking about these resentments in greater detail with impartial others to better understand the nature of the resentments and what you need to say. Try to discuss resentments descriptively and non-judgmentally, and allow yourself to feel the pain attached to them. Do not amplify your emotions, but also do not attempt to minimize their impacts on you. You may consider journaling as an alternative to or as an initial step toward talking with someone. If expressing the resentments will likely overwhelm you, make sure you are in a safe environment and in Wise and Clear Mind.

After journaling and/or discussing resentments, choose one that you may want to address. Take on resentments one at a time. Specifically decide what you want to say to the person or people relative to your chosen resentment. Remember your FAST skills, especially being fair and grounded in values, and how you can use GIVE along with what will essentially be a DEAR MAN. Write a script and rehearse it with someone. Anticipate how your DEAR MAN, even done skillfully with GIVE, will be received. *Remember to own your contributions to the situations that caused the resentment and include that in the script.*

After you finish this preparation, make a final decision about whether you want to address the resentment directly. Discussing resentments with the people involved works when you anticipate that they will be receptive. *In general, avoid directly discussing resentments with people who would likely react in a way that harms you and with people who would likely be harmed by the discussion.* In these situations, writing a letter that you will not mail, journaling, or talking to an open chair (i.e., Clint Eastwood-ing) can be a healing outlet.

When you have clear interpersonal and distress tolerance plans along with sufficient behavioral rehearsal, reach out to set up a time to talk. Consider the timing and other factors to set the discussion up for success. Keep in mind the qualities of being assertive: Your goal is to skillfully discuss the resentment.

The ultimate goal of addressing resentments in one way or another is acceptance and forgiveness, so you can be free to move forward. The preparation and conversation can be stressful, but the reward will likely be worth it.

Resentments Worksheet ————————————————————

Use this exercise to learn more about your resentments and to begin the process of addressing them.

Describe a resentment related to another person in detail and in non-judgmental language:

Describe your behaviors that contributed to the resentment:

Describe what your goal(s) are for addressing the resentment (if you choose to do so):

Describe what you would like to say to the other person using GIVE and DEAR MAN (use another sheet of paper if necessary):

Describe in more detail your plan for addressing this resentment (if you choose to do so), including the skills you will need to practice:

Using Interpersonal Effectiveness to Make Amends

Substance use and other ineffective behaviors can result in harm to other people in both direct and indirect ways. The pain and suffering you may have caused others through your actions (and inactions) may create pain and suffering for you as well. The guilt and shame that results from harming others can directly keep people in the cycle of addiction or make them vulnerable to relapse by allowing for escape and avoidance of these emotions.

Not addressing the harm caused to others also interferes with recovery. For example, you may think you need to continue to avoid those you have hurt, closing your world rather than opening it. Additionally, ignoring the need to make amends allows you to ignore the negative effects of substance use (or other behavior), creating another barrier to your recovery.

Making amends begins with openly acknowledging the behaviors that harmed other people. What did you do, and who did it affect? With this acknowledgement comes emotion, and you need to experience it without amplifying it or minimizing it. The emotion honors the relative seriousness of what was done. Balance experiencing any intense emotion with distress tolerance skills, and consider if you need to do this work in a safe environment.

One part of making amends is apologizing for the specific actions that affected others, clearly recognizing the impacts of those actions. If a direct apology cannot be made (i.e., if it would cause further harm), then it can be helpful to write a letter that you will not mail, to journal, or to talk to an open chair.

However, amends go far beyond an apology. An important part of amends is repairing the situation to the best of your ability. For example, if you stole money or property, you would pay it back or return it. Justice is restored through restitution that honors the pain and loss that resulted from your actions. If you cannot make amends for a practical reason (e.g., you cannot or should not contact the affected person, you literally do not have the means to restore the situation), then you may have to make symbolic amends, often through committing to touch the lives of others in positive ways. Dialectically, this makes meaning out of something that was terrible.

Truly making amends is about changing your life so that you no longer fall into the same mistakes that caused others harm; it is about pursuing health, wellness, and recovery. It is about working skills to live a life grounded in values and your true intentions.

Although the process of making amends is focused on and for others, you can enjoy the freedom that ultimately comes from sincere efforts.

Making Amends Worksheet ────────────────────

Use this exercise to begin the process of making amends.

Describe in detail and in non-judgmental language the behavior that harmed someone else and who that person is:

Describe in detail and in non-judgmental language how you believe that person was affected by your behavior, including the emotional impact:

Describe the apology you would like to make, taking responsibility for your behavior and making no excuses:

Describe how you plan to repair the situation, in real and symbolic ways:

Describe your commitment to making changes in your life to avoid the same mistake:

Source Citations for Modules and Skills

Mindfulness Module (Linehan, 1993b)

Wise Mind (Linehan, 1993b)

What Skills (Linehan, 1993b)

How Skills (Linehan, 1993b)

Addict Mind, Clean Mind, and Clear Mind (Dimeff and Linehan, 2008)

Distress Tolerance Module (Linehan, 1993b)

ACCEPTS (Linehan, 1993b)

Self-Soothe (Linehan, 1993b; expanded by Pederson, 2011)

Urge Surfing (Marlatt & Gordon, 1985)

Bridge Burning (Linehan, unpublished; published by Pederson, 2011)

IMPROVE the Moment (Linehan, 1993b)

Pros and Cons (Linehan, 1993b)

Grounding Yourself (Pederson, 2011)

Radical Acceptance (Linehan, 1993b)

Everyday Acceptance (Pederson, 2011)

Willingness (Linehan, 1993b)

Emotion Regulation Module (Linehan, 1993b)

PLEASE/PLEASED (Linehan, 1993b; adapted by Pederson, 2011)

Build Positive Experience (Linehan, 1993b)

Attend to Relationships (Eboni Webb, unpublished; published by Pederson, 2011)

Mood Momentum (Pederson, 2011)

Opposite to Emotion (Linehan, 1993b)

Interpersonal Effectiveness Module (Linehan, 1993b)

FAST (Linehan, 1993b)

GIVE/GIVE (Linehan, 1993b; adapted by Pederson, 2011)

VALIDATION (Pederson, 2011)

DEAR MAN (Linehan, 1993b)

Bibliography

American Psychological Association. (2005). *Report of the 2005 Presidential Task Force on evidence-based practice*. Retrieved 1-3-2010 from http://www.apa.org/practice/ebpreport.pdf.

Beauchamp, T.C. & Childress, J.F. (2001). *Principles of biomedical ethics*. New York: The Oxford Press.

Clarkin, J. F., Levy, K. N., Lenzenweger, M. F., & Kernberg, O. F. (2007). Evaluating three treatments for borderline personality disorder: A multiwave study. *The American Journal of Psychiatry, 164*, 922–928.

Connors, G.J., Donovan, D. M., & DiClemente, C.C. (2001). *Substance abuse treatment and the stages of change*. New York: The Guilford Press.

DeFife, J.A. & Hilsenroth, M.J. (2011). Starting off on the right foot: Common elements in early psychotherapy process. *Journal of Psychotherapy Integration, Vol. 21, No. 2*, 172-191.

Dimeff, L. A., & Koerner, K. (2007). *Dialectical behavior therapy in clinical practice: Applications across disorders and settings*. New York: The Guilford Press.

Dimeff, L.A., & Linehan, M.M. (2008). Dialectical behavior therapy for substance abusers. *Addiction Science & Clinical Practice*, June; 4(2): 39-47.

Dimeff, L.A., & Linehan, M.M. (2012). *Dialectical behavior therapy for substance abusers*. www.all-about-psychology.com/psychology-on-kindle.html.

Duncan, B., Miller, S., Wampold, B., & Hubble, M. (2010). *The heart and soul of change: Delivering what works in therapy, 2nd ed*. Washington, D. C.: American Psychological Association.

Finley, J.R. & Lenz, B.S. (2009). *Addiction treatment homework planner*. Hoboken: John Wiley & Sons, Inc.

Frank, J.D. & Frank, J.B. (1991). *Persuasion and healing: A comparative study of psychotherapy (3rd ed.)*. Baltimore: John Hopkins University Press.

Hayes, S. C., Strosahl, K. D., & Houts, A. (Eds.) (1999). *A practical guide to acceptance and commitment therapy*. New York: Springer.

Kazdin, A.E. (2008). Evidence-based treatment and practice: New opportunities to bridge clinical research and practice, enhance the knowledge base, and improve patient care. *American Psychologist*, Vol. 63, No. 3, 146-159.

Koerner, K. (2012). *Doing dialectical behavior therapy*. New York: The Guilford Press.

Kübler-Ross, E. (2005) *On grief and grieving: Finding the meaning of grief through the five stages of loss*. New York: Scribner.

Linehan, M. M. (1997). Validation and psychotherapy. In A. Bohart & L. Greenberg (Eds.), *Empathy reconsidered: New directions in psychotherapy* (pp. 353-392). Washington, D.C.: American Psychological Association.

Linehan, M. M. (1993a). *Cognitive-behavioral treatment of borderline personality disorder*. New York: The Guilford Press.

Linehan, M. M. (1993b). *Skills training manual for treating borderline personality disorder*. New York: The Guilford Press.

Marlatt, G.A., & Gordon, J.R. (1985). *Relapse prevention: Maintenance strategies in the treatment of addictive behaviors*. New York: The Guilford Press.

Marra, T. (2004). *Depressed & anxious: The dialectical behavior therapy workbook for overcoming depression and anxiety.* Oakland: New Harbinger Press.

Marra, T. (2005). *Dialectical behavior therapy in private practice: A practical and comprehensive guide.* Oakland: New Harbinger Press.

McMann, S., Sayrs, J.H., Dimeff, L.A., & Linehan, MM (2007). Dialectical behavior therapy for individuals with borderline personality disorder and substance dependence. In Dimeff, L. A., & Koerner, K. (Eds). *Dialectical behavior therapy in clinical practice: Applications across disorders and settings.* New York: The Guilford Press.

Miller, W.R. & Rollnick, S. (2002). *Motivational interviewing: Preparing people for change.* New York: The Guilford Press.

Moonshine, C. (2008). *Acquiring competency & achieving proficiency with dialectical behavior therapy: Volume I - The clinician's guidebook.* Eau Claire: PESI.

Moonshine, C. (2008). *Acquiring competency & achieving proficiency with dialectical behavior therapy: Volume II - The worksheets.* Eau Claire: PESI.

Muesler, K.T., Noordsy, D.L., Drake, R.E., & Fox, L. (2003). *Integrated treatment for dual disorders: A guide to effective practice.* New York: The Guilford Press.

Pederson, L. & Sidwell Pederson, C. (2012). *The expanded dialectical behavior therapy skills training manual: Practical DBT for self-help and individual & group treatment settings.* Eau Claire: Premier Publishing & Media.

Prochaska, J. O. & DiClemente, C. (1983). Stages and processes of self-change of smoking: Toward and integrative model of change. *Journal of Consulting and Clinical Psychology, 51,* 390-395.

Prochaska, J. O., DiClemente, C., & Norcross (1992). In search of how people change: Applications to addictive behaviors. *American Psychologist, 47,* 1102-1114.

Prochaska, J. O., Norcross, J., & DiClemente, C. (2006). *Changing for good: A revolutionary six-stage program for overcoming bad habits and moving your life positively forward.* New York: Harper Collins.

Soler, J. Trujols, J. Pascual, J.C., Portella, M.J., Barrachina, J. Campins, J. Tejedor, R., Alvarez, E. & Perez, V. (2008). Stages of change in dialectical behaviour therapy for borderline personality disorder. *British Journal of Clinical Psychology, 47,* 417-426.

Substance Abuse and Mental Health Services Administration (SAMHSA) (2010). *Integrated Treatment for Co-Occurring Disorders Evidence-Based Practices (EBP) KIT.* Retrieved 6-1-2012 from http:// store.samhsa.gov/product/ Integrated-Treatment.../SMA08-4367

Wampold, B. E. (2001). *The great psychotherapy debate: Models, methods, and findings.* New Jersey: Lawrence Erlbaum Associates.

Weinberg, I., Ronningstam, E., Goldblatt, M.J., Schechter, M., & Maltsberger, J.T. (2011). Common factors in empirically supported treatments of borderline personality disorder. *Current Psychiatry Reports,* 13:60-68

Webb, C. A., DeRubeis, R. J., & Barber, J. P. (2010). Therapist adherence/competence and treatment outcome: A meta-analytic review. *Journal of Consulting and Clinical Psychology,* 78(2), 200–211.

38651806R00097

Made in the USA
Lexington, KY
19 January 2015